INTIMACY AND INTELLIGIBILITY

INTIMACY and INTELLIGIBILITY

WORD AND LIFE IN AUGUSTINE'S
DE MAGISTRO

ERIKA KIDD

University of Notre Dame Press
Notre Dame, Indiana

Library of Congress Control Number: 2025934552

ISBN: 978-0-268-21021-2 (Hardback)
ISBN: 978-0-268-21023-6 (WebPDF)
ISBN: 978-0-268-21024-3(Epub3)

GPSR Compliance Inquiries:
Lightning Source France, 1 Av. Johannes Gutenberg, 78310 Maurepas, France
compliance@lightningsource.fr | Phone: +33 1 30 49 23 42

CONTENTS

ACKNOWLEDGMENTS

My first teacher of Augustine, Carl Vaught, taught me that philosophy always begins in story. I am unable to take the measure of the ways Augustine's story has carried me, personally and professionally, but I am grateful.
Jim Wetzel, my dear friend and teacher over the last two decades, introduced me to *De magistro* and has helped me see, again and again, why it is
worthy of attention. Many others have inspired my engagement with Augustine, including Catherine Conybeare, William Desmond, John Peter
Kenney, and Kathleen Skerrett. Edmund Bloedow, Jeff Fish, and Amy Vail
made me into a Latinist. Edith Humphrey and David Jeffrey taught me
how to read with charity.

This book was nourished at several stages by the work of the Augustinian Institute at Villanova University. A portion of the research was completed during my time as Patricia H. Imbesi Fellow under the auspices of
the institute. I am grateful for the vision of the late Fr. Tom Martin, OSA,
inaugural director of the institute, and for the work of those who have
taken up the torch: Jim Wetzel, Paul Camacho, Fr. Allan Fitzgerald, OSA,
Ian Clausen, and Colleen Murphy. Those folks, together with Veronica
Roberts Ogle, Terence Sweeney, Patricia Grosse, and others, have wel-
comed me into a vibrant scholarly community, where I have glimpsed the
beata vita Augustine and Adeodatus describe.

I could not ask for better colleagues than I found in Catholic Studies at
the University of St. Thomas. Billy Junker generously read many chapters,
saw exactly what I wanted to do, and helped me do it better. John Boyle
and Fr. Austin Litke, OP, were always up for Augustinian conversation.

Others protected my time and space so I could write. Three University of St. Thomas Faculty Development grants funded portions of my research and writing. Special thanks are due to the graduate students in my Augustine seminars who helped me work out some of the ideas in the book.

My writing partners, Miriel Thomas Reneau and Charlie Gillespie, saw me through the muddy patches with good cheer and courage. Danny Dalenberg helped with many details. Bob Land edited the manuscript with great care. Emily King, my editor at University of Notre Dame Press, was a careful shepherd of the project. My heartfelt thanks go to Karmen MacKendrick and Michael Foley, my external reviewers, who saw why this book matters.

Finally, I offer a word of thanks to my family. My parents, Bruce and Eunice Bassler, have been wonderfully supportive of my work and have faithfully directed my attention to the voice of Christ the teacher. My boys, Teddy, John Walter, and Samuel, have shown me what moves the heart to speak. I love each of them with all my heart. My deepest gratitude, though, goes to my beloved husband, David. My best critic, he often understands my words better than I do. He made time for my work in more ways than one, and he encouraged me in my labors when things got tough. This book is the fruit of a lifetime's conversation with him, and I can't wait for more.

INTRODUCTION

The past two decades have seen a surge of interest in Augustine's early dialogues. Recent scholarship gives overdue attention both to the arguments and to the dramatic staging of these dialogues.[1] Yet amid that surge, Augustine's *De magistro*, a North African dialogue from just after the Cassiciacum period, remains only superficially studied. *De magistro* takes place in Thagaste around 389, and presents a conversation between Augustine and his teenage son Adeodatus on the question (*mag.* 1.1): "What do we want to accomplish when we speak with one another?"[2] The fact that it has been overlooked and misunderstood may owe something to the text's odd ambitions and construction. *De magistro* is a curious mélange. It is, first and foremost, a record of a real conversation, full of the jokes, hints, guesses, confusions, quotations, and insights spoken by Augustine and Adeodatus. It is also a subtle work of philosophy and theology, examining topics ranging from signs and signification to Christ, the inner teacher, and blending flights of abstract thought with concrete talk about how and why human beings speak. The text also serves, Augustine tells us in his *Confessiones*, as a memorial for Adeodatus, who died unexpectedly not long after the conversation took place. What *De magistro* is and what it does is not easy to say.

The dialogue unfolds as an extended meditation on the opening question "What do we want to accomplish when we speak with one another?" and spends a good deal of time exploring the suggestion that we talk *primarily to inform one another*. Yet there is a trick to this dialogue, one largely overlooked by its few commentators, who tend to strip out the so-called philosophical content of the dialogue from its conversational and familial context. Such commentators take Augustine at his initial word—that we speak to inform one another—and they suggest that Augustine means to propose and solve a skeptical problem of meaning.[3] They suggest Augustine rather impressively anticipates modern questions like, "How can I be sure another mind knows what I mean to signify when I speak?" and "How can I know the words I speak with others are meaningful rather than meaningless?" Yet when the problem is cast in these terms, Augustine's apparent solution in the figure of Christ, the inner teacher who speaks truth to the knowing mind, seems odd and ad hoc. Contemporary philosophers, fascinated by Augustine's early casting of the skeptical problem of meaning, are less impressed by his mediocre theory of epistemology. If Augustine's apparent solution to the skeptical problem of meaning is so unsatisfying, however, it is time to reevaluate whether supplying such a solution is the point of the dialogue. My own view is that Augustine does not propose the view that we talk to inform in order to recommend it, but to show its flaws and to draw his son and his readers into something richer. A careful rereading of De magistro is long overdue.

This book undertakes such a reading, rooted in my conviction that De magistro is not a text about informing, but a text about intimacy. I argue that the primary aim of the dialogue is not to resolve a skeptical problem nor to help readers become more skilled at using words to inform the minds of others by relying on Christ, the inner teacher, as a cosmic accomplice. I offer a fresh reading of the inner teacher as one who binds father and son together in an intimate shared space of meaning, a space open to possibilities of misapprehension and loss, and formed by the life they share. Yet I do not begin with these conclusions. Instead I imitate Augustine's own practice in the dialogue, starting with the problematic view about speaking and examining what makes that view so tempting. The view that we speak primarily to inform turns out to be wrongheaded, but also deeply attractive, and Augustine dramatizes the allure of that view, even as he weans his son from it. The dialogue, a form of therapy, helps Adeodatus and Augustine (and their readers) practice new habits of thought and activity, particularly with respect to how they conceive of the blessed life. De magistro turns out to be a spiritual exercise, aimed at the purification and formation of the intelligence and the heart.

I admit there is a whiff of controversy in my claim that this book is a reading of Augustine's *De magistro*. I do not aim to resolve what many have identified as the central problem of the dialogue. I do not give a line-by-line commentary on the text. I also give attention to texts that are not *De magistro*. Not everyone who sets out to write about this dialogue would go about it as I have. Therefore it is useful to begin with a brief account of the distinctive features of my reading and my approach to the text.

First, my reading tries to escape the prevailing modern methodology that shapes much of the scholarship on *De magistro*. Though my work on the dialogue is grounded in and informed by contemporary Augustinian scholarship on *De magistro*, it was clear to me that a broader cast of characters—overlooked mothers, forgotten lovers, lonely children, and magisterial fathers—was needed to stage my reading of the dialogue. Because much of the scholarship of *De magistro* is rooted in a set of broadly modern concerns about clarity, control, and skepticism, I enlisted a postmodern ally, Luce Irigaray, to help me interrogate Augustine's late antique text. Irigaray's retelling of the myths of Dionysus, Apollo, and Christ in *Marine Lover* exposes the disincarnating bias of the modern methodology and helps me to recover and illuminate the central concerns of *De magistro*. Irigaray's text helps reveal the patriarchal roots and theological implications of the temptation Augustine describes. Augustine's questions find fruitful resonance within Irigaray's text and cast of characters, and my engagement with her text puts flesh on some key ideas and figures from Augustine's dialogue. Following Irigaray's lead, I also have tried to be attentive to the women who lurk in the shadows of *De magistro*: the mother of Adeodatus, Monica, Lady Continence, and Mary, the Mother of God. Consequently, I make use of several relevant passages from the *Confessiones* and the Gospel of Luke to tell their stories. Each of these figures, in different ways, helps us to understand what intimacy might look like.

Second, my reading of the dialogue is attentive to its literary form. That form matters, and understanding it is a vital part of understanding the dialogue. My interest in *De magistro* developed during the months I spent translating the text for a Latin exam in graduate school. That translation work heightened my attention to the drama of the text and to those aspects of the dialogue that contain meaning apart from what can be captured by standard philosophical propositions. As I discovered through my labors with the Latin, the book is a record of a real human conversation, full of inside jokes, confusion, teasing, reminiscence, earnest explanations, and dropped threads. While the written account of the conversation may not be an exact account of each word spoken, Augustine says all the opinions attributed to Adeodatus in the written dialogue come from the young man himself. Putting Augustine's Latin words into my own tongue enlivened my attention to Augustine's careful staging of the dialogue and to his word-plays and images, some of which the existing English translations obscure. My translation work revealed to me the human quality of the conversation. It is concrete and familial, and those features are part of its significance, no less than the theories father and son entertain. Though it is not devoid of theorizing, *De magistro* is no textbook, nor merely an account of a theory of language.[4] Instead the dialogue reveals, above all, the relationship between the two men, father and son.

Third, my reading is attentive to Augustine's interest in his son's (and his readers') desire or motivation in speaking. He asks, "What do we *want* to accomplish when we speak?" Do we want to inform? To be informed? Though Augustine posed the question to his son, his question resonated with me quite deeply, as I taught undergraduate and graduate students, taught my children to speak, gave academic presentations, and spoke with others in a variety of contexts. Augustine's *we* in the opening question refers most immediately and obviously to Adeodatus and Augustine, but the question of desire and the temptations and insights they entertain are not unique to those two. They are universal, and we readers of Augustine's text can find ourselves in them too. Augustine's *we* invites you and me to interrogate our own desire and thereby participate in the spiritual exercise of the dialogue. I have adopted what I take to be Augustine's invitational use of the word *we*, and I use it often in this book to refer to Augustine, Adeodatus, and to us, the readers of *De magistro*. I hope my use of that term invites my reader to enter Augustine's questions, self-examination, and deeper attentiveness to the presence of the divine life.

Fourth, my reading is attentive to Augustine's assurance to Adeodatus that their conversation about words is a preparation for entering into the beata vita, the blessed life. Augustine describes that entering as a parturition, using the Latin term *parturire*. This oft-overlooked metaphor of birth is an indispensable interpretive key and has shaped my approach to the dialogue from beginning to end. The conversation in *De magistro* begins with some strange contractions of language and ends with the life of Christ—the life that Augustine hopes he and Adeodatus might enter more fully. Augustine's metaphor, to which I recur at several points in this book, roots my conviction that *De magistro* is not primarily an account of a theory of language but a meditation on living the blessed life. This insight frames how we might understand Christ, the inner teacher, not as a guarantor of meaning, but as the life shared by father and son, a life that abides and holds them together. Though neither knew at the time just how liminal and close to death their conversation was, much of it could come back to Augustine as consolation after the untimely death of Adeodatus. The desire Augustine tries to cultivate in his son is, above all, a desire for heaven. Whatever they are seeking through their conversation, it is not trivial.

I divide my reading of *De magistro* into two parts, each of which contains several chapters. In part 1, "Informers," I examine Augustine's provisional insistence that we speak primarily to inform, and I explain why that view is both tempting and misguided. Throughout part 1, I imitate Augustine's practice of dramatizing not only the appeal of the view that we speak to inform but also its breakdown. Chapter 1, "Informing," examines Augustine's initial insistence in *De magistro* that we talk only to inform one another, using words to sign our meanings to each other. Adeodatus is more resistant to the strange claim than most of the dialogue's commentators are, but Augustine presses forward, wearing down Adeodatus's hesitancy and securing his agreement. Though the claim has some plausibility, I show that it quickly leads father and son into strange consequences and inconsistencies, including the odd conclusion that human beings have no reason to talk with God. In this chapter, I also try to show the appeal of thinking that we talk primarily to inform. It is a legitimately tempting view, seeming to solve certain difficulties about our speaking together.

Chapter 2, "Prelude," takes up two moments of breakdown resulting from Augustine and Adeodatus's provisional commitment to the thesis that we speak to inform. The thesis, rather than enhancing their ability to communicate, seems to diminish and contract that ability. I argue that Augustine's commitment to the thesis nonetheless has a pedagogical point. Augustine calls their conversation an exercise, and I explain how the exercise prepares father and son to enter the blessed life by intentionally revealing the tension between their theorizing and their actual way of speaking together.

In chapter 3, "Gods," I draw on Luce Irigaray's mythic meditation on the births of the gods to examine the patriarchal valence of using words primarily to inform. Irigaray retells the stories of the births of Dionysus, Apollo, and Christ, framing them as disincarnating ideals of communication. Her text reveals how talking to inform is bound up with problematic ideas of eternity, and I use her stories to sketch a portrait of an inner teacher who serves as a flawless informer—a tempting but corrupt idol of communication.

In part 2, "Intimates," I argue that De magistro is a text about speaking within a form of intimacy, a shared inner space of meaning. To flesh out this claim, I examine examples of intimacy from De magistro, Confessiones, and Marine Lover: parent-child intimacy, the intimacy of lovers, and the intimacy between God and the soul. Chapter 4, "Deliverance," is an extended examination of the pivotal moment in De magistro where Augustine proposes to his son that their conversation about signs is an act of parturition, a site of deliverance into the beata vita. In response to the disincarnating view that we speak to inform the minds of others, I suggest that the beata vita is no rejection of incarnate human life, but its perfection. Drawing on passages from Confessiones, I argue that intelligibility cannot exist apart from intimacy and connection with bodies, loves, times, and histories. Augustine's intimacy with God in Christ recalls the fullness and plenitude of the saint's life in the flesh. He invites Adeodatus into a similar form of intimacy with Christ, the inner teacher.

The image of Christ is underdetermined—intentionally so—in De magistro. In chapter 5, "Mother of the Word," I return to Irigaray's meditation on Christ and his mother in order to lay the groundwork for my discussion of Christ, the inner teacher, in the following chapter. In both De magistro and Irigaray's Marine Lover, the occlusion of feminine figures is tied up with the desire to talk to inform. As this book moves, following Augustine's lead, beyond that thesis, I reintroduce the figure of Mary, Christ's mother. She shows us what intimacy with Christ, the inner teacher, looks like. Christ the Word, child of his divine Father and his mortal mother, comes to life in the context of intimacy and desire. De magistro reminds us that our own words come to life in a similar way.

Chapter 6, "Christ's Life," presents two portraits of Christ, the inner teacher, drawn from the end of *De magistro* and from Augustine's conversation with Monica at Ostia in *Confessiones* 9. I argue that Augustine's inner teacher does not serve to contract the sphere of meaning, making communication less ambiguous and more clear. Instead Augustine's inner teacher draws interlocutors into the life of Christ, a life that is not an alternative to nor replacement for the life they live together. I argue that the inner teacher of *De magistro* is inner because it is intimate, circumscribing a shared space of meaning. Augustine's metaphor of interiority suggests not an inward citadel but something more like harboring another in one's heart.

The final chapter of the book, "Words, Afterward," draws out the significance of the untimely death of Adeodatus, not long after the conversation recorded in *De magistro*. Talking to inform is a way of trying to speak beyond the possibilities of loss, by grounding meaning in what is universal, disembodied, and abstract. Augustine's book refuses this cold consolation. Instead *De magistro*, a meditation on the intimate connection between words and life, is a memorial to the love and life he has shared with his son.

Though there is something mistaken about the conviction that we talk only to inform, Augustine knows the mistake is not a stupid one. It cuts right to the heart of our disincarnating illusions about what it is to communicate with one another. As we make our way with words, again and again we are tempted to try to get a fix on meaning and to exorcise ambiguity, indeterminacy, and the general messiness of finite human lives, forgetting that such an exorcism, if successful, might leave our linguistic exchanges devoid of any real meaning. The curious thing is that our words often belie such efforts. They allow us to say much less and much more than we mean. Augustine's metaphor of pregnancy and birth does not suggest we will be able to perfect or manage our words. It promises instead that our speaking together offers the richest kind of deliverance—not just out of a cramped way with words, but into a life most blessed.

PART 1

INFORMERS

CHAPTER ONE

INFORMING

The trajectory of *De magistro* is set by Augustine's opening question to his son (*mag.* 1.1): "What do we want to accomplish when we speak with one another?"[1] The question is both philosophical and poignant. It might seem to raise an airy question along the lines of "What do words do?" or "What is the reason for speaking?" But spoken from father to the teenage Adeodatus, the question takes on a personal tone too: "Why do we—you and I—speak together?" Why does Augustine speak with Adeodatus? Why does Adeodatus speak with his father? What desire motivates their exchange of words? What do they want? Augustine's question is not simply about *any* exchange of words. It is also about *this* exchange of words, in the dialogue, with his gifted teenage son. Augustine's question skates across the distinction between the personal and the philosophical.

De magistro records a real conversation between Augustine and Adeodatus. Augustine's evocative question immediately draws the reader into reflection as well. His question is directed toward Adeodatus, but it is also directed at the reader. Augustine wrote the conversation down after all. The dialogue form invites the reader to be not a philosophical voyeur but an engaged conversation partner. *What do we want to accomplish when we speak with one another?* The question is first and foremost a question about desire. What do we *want* in speaking together? Are we trying to get something? Make something? Accomplish something? Augustine invites us to notice our own desire but also the desire of the one with whom we are speaking. We talk all the time. Unreflectively, we suppose we know why we do it. But have we really noticed what we do with words and why? Augustine tells his son—and us—that this question is worth our attention.

Adeodatus, whose keen mind and filial love are in evidence throughout the dialogue, has two ready answers. He says they speak to inform (*docere*) or to be informed (*discere*) (*mag.* 1.1). In English translations of the dialogue, these terms are universally translated as to teach (*docere*) and to learn (*discere*).[2] While these are standard translations of the Latin, what Augustine describes in the dialogue is better captured by the more capacious terms of *informing* (*docere*) and *being informed* (*discere*). For Augustine, not all *docere* is intentional; not all *discere* is active. Sometimes we inform without (intentionally) teaching while at other times we are informed without making any effort to learn. Our attempts to teach and to learn are often ineffectual. Nonetheless, we continue to inform and be informed.

Adeodatus's answers are intuitive, if incomplete. We often do want to inform and be informed when we speak. For example, several years ago, my husband used words to inform me that he had added vanilla and cinnamon to our chicken stir-fry dinner, and I used words to find out why he had done such an unappetizing thing. Teachers inform students about the details of historical events. Siblings inform each other about the locations of hidden Christmas presents. Pedestrians give directions to drivers. Parents tell toddlers stoves are hot. In such ways and more, we use words to exchange or receive information. We speak to inform and be informed.

On second thought, however, we would surely say Adeodatus has given a strangely limited account of what we do with words. His list of motivations for speaking should be much expanded. I do not aim to inform or to be informed when I say, "It sure is a nice day today," to someone who knows full well what the weather is. I do not talk to inform or be informed when I say something poetic like, "'Twas brillig, and the slithy toves / Did gyre and gimble in the wabe."[3] Nor do I desire to inform or be informed when I tell my husband I love him or make a self-deprecating joke to cheer him up. It is easy to come up with many motivations for speaking that do not fit within the categories that Adeodatus mentions.

Augustine agrees with Adeodatus's claim that we speak to inform. Yet, bizarrely, he calls into question his son's suggestion that we speak to be informed or to learn. Even asking questions of others—which might appear to be an instance of speaking to learn—is shown to be a version of speaking to inform. For when we put a question to someone, Augustine explains, we inform that person what we want, that is, to be given some piece of information (*mag.* 1.1). My question to my fishmonger about how to cook branzino is, on this view, an attempt to inform him of my desire to know that information. Augustine makes Adeodatus's already narrow account even narrower, and Adeodatus's intuition that we talk to be informed drops from consideration for the bulk of the dialogue.

The view Augustine defends at this point is quite simple: we speak only to inform. Unfortunately, as both experience and the dialogue teach us, we are frustratingly unsuccessful at using words to inform others. This is true not just for contingent reasons like a hearer's failure to pay attention or a speaker's failure to say what she means. The impossibility of using words to inform is part of the nature of language. It turns out Augustine knows this full well. While he spends the first half of the dialogue arguing that no one can be informed without words, he ultimately makes a complete about-face, arguing in the latter part of the dialogue that words cannot inform (or teach) anyone anything. We speak to inform, but our words do not perform the very function we want them to perform. Augustine tells his son,

> The most credit I would give to words is this: they summon us to seek and know a thing, but they do not make a thing known. The one who teaches me presents to my eyes or to any bodily sense or to my mind those things I want to know. From words, we learn nothing but words—just their sound and noise. For since things that are not signs cannot be words, when I have heard a word, I don't even know whether it is a word, until I know what it signifies.[4]

We get knowledge from things, not from words. It is not that words *sometimes* fail to bring others to knowledge. They *never* accomplish this. They cannot. It may look like the dialogue's first moral is that it is naïve to suppose we can use words to inform or be informed. The desire expressed in the opening pages—to speak to inform—looks doomed to failure.

In Augustine's demonstration of the impossibility of using words to inform, the modest body of scholarship on *De magistro* locates the emergence of a skeptical problem of meaning. Most commentators breeze past Adeodatus's good intuition that we might speak for different kinds of reasons.[5]

Instead they take up Augustine's suggestion that we talk primarily to in-form, while adding a set of modern concerns about the difficulty or impos-sibility of informing another.[6] Their worry is that no collection of words, gestures, or other signs can ever *guarantee* the conveyance of meaning. We may try to inform someone by using our words to signal meanings, but we can never know we have succeeded. We can never be sure we have spoken words free from ambiguity and the possibility of misapprehension. This speaks not to our failure but to the inadequacy of words, the only tools we have been given for the job. No words can ever serve to fix the mind of an-other on some meaning. Even under the best of circumstances in the easiest of conversations, there is no certainty that my interlocutor and I are moved to contemplate the same reality when we hear a word spoken. There is no guarantee of intelligibility.

On this skeptical picture, the body looks like an obstacle to communi-cation, for it seems to impede full access to the minds of others. The body also seems to limit access to an intelligible realm wherein two minds might connect through contemplation of some object of knowledge. If the episte-mological ideal is two minds fixed on the exact same reality, no such ideal can be realized in this finite, mortal life. Instead, the mundane reality is this: What I mean is clear and present in my mind; what you mean is clear and present in yours. We each have access to our own meanings, and words cannot be relied upon to inform you of mine. Not only can I not know with perfect certainty that you and I understand the same thing when we hear a trivial word like *cup* but neither can I know we understand the same thing when we speak to each other using words like *promise* or *love*. If our bodies separate us into two discrete points of view, I am always closer to my meanings than other people are. The body blocks meaning and connection with others. Or so the skeptical picture proposes.

If the skeptical problem is the animating issue of *De magistro*, Au-gustine's notions of the inner teacher (Christ) and the *beata vita* (heaven) may appear to be solutions to the problem. If the possibilities of human communication are bleak, perhaps the inner teacher speaks inner words that can reach places merely human words cannot. If the realm of human speech is dim and uncertain, perhaps the beata vita promises escape into brighter visions of perfect understanding. Perhaps Augustine gets his idea of the divine Word out of disillusionment with merely human words. The framing of the problem forms the solution we seek. If we think our problem with words is a skeptical problem of meaning, the solution will be some guarantee of intelligibility, allowing us to escape the opacity the body seems to interpose between us. In this kind of solution, God fulfills our desire to use words to inform by rectifying the deficiencies of merely human communication. Our attempts to inform are doomed to failure, but God can succeed where our words fail.

While this is a tidy picture, the view that *De magistro* is concerned with describing and solving a skeptical problem of meaning is a substantial misinterpretation of the dialogue. The view rests on the problematic assumption that the goal of the dialogue remains the same from first to last: to show that speaking is all about informing. This problematic assumption leads to misreadings of key features of the dialogue, including the role of the inner teacher, the beata vita, and the value of incarnate life. Nonetheless, since the skeptical problem of meaning is the issue that has most exercised commentators on the dialogue, it is where we will start. Augustine begins his dialogue with the (mistaken) view that we talk primarily to inform. We, likewise, begin this book with a version of that mistaken view.

Toward the end of *De magistro*, Augustine invokes the inner teacher, whom he describes as "truth which keeps vigil over the mind." That truth is Christ, who lives in the inner man and who teaches us there. Augustine terms him both "the immutable power of God" and "everlasting wisdom." He writes, "Every reasoning spirit turns to him."[7] When someone speaks, Augustine explains, we understand not by turning our attention to words themselves, but rather to the teacher who speaks inwardly to each of us. In these passages, some readers detect an early hint of what comes to be termed Augustine's theory of illumination, where Christ's illumination of the mind allows the mind to know, just as physical illumination allows the eye to see. One scholar writes that, for Augustine, "divine illumination enacts the possibility of the teaching and learning, which would not otherwise be possible."[8] That possibility comes from a created intellectual capacity perfected and restored through faith.[9]

Some readers take it that Christ, the one true teacher, is Augustine's solution to the so-called skeptical problem of meaning. While Augustine and Adeodatus spend much of *De magistro* discussing how signs teach, the mention of the inner teacher comes toward the end, shortly after Augustine introduces the possibility that speakers and hearers are in fact not taught by signs at all. Father and son agree that signs cannot teach us because a sign cannot itself reveal what it signifies. A sign is only a sign for us if we already know the thing it signifies. Therefore, words cannot inform others, as we desire them to. In the face of this apparent breakdown of human signification, some commentators have suggested it is Christ who allows interlocutors to be informed when words are spoken. The troubling paradox of signs, writes one commentator, is solved by Christ: "Our teacher is truth itself, which governs our minds by showing us things as they are and so enabling us rightly to use and interpret signs."[10]

While philosophers have been drawn to Augustine's interesting framing of the skeptical problem, most are hesitant about adopting what they take to be Augustine's theological solution, the inner teacher.[11] One translator writes, "Nor need we accept (or even explore!) Augustine's theory of illumination to take the important point from his discussion, namely that learning (and so teaching) pose a deep and puzzling *philosophical* problem."[12] Read this way, the dialogue reinforces a split between philosophy and theology, where Augustine dazzles at the former before getting mired in the latter.

In his address "Wittgenstein and Augustine *De Magistro*," an essay that has arguably done the most to set the terms of the contemporary discussion of the dialogue, Myles Burnyeat highlights the common ground between Augustine's and Ludwig Wittgenstein's observation that no outward display of signs can ever guarantee the delivery of an intended meaning.[13] For both thinkers, signs (including words) cannot inform minds, at least not reliably. One body's difference from another makes speaking into so much gesturing from within mental silos. To Burnyeat's ear, Augustine articulates an ancient problem of understanding with a modern resonance, by marrying a Platonic sense of the complexity of understanding to a modern sense of skepticism.

For Augustine, says Burnyeat, teaching (*docere*) is "imparting knowledge."[14] Therefore, to ask whether teaching is possible is to ask "whether one human being can bring another to know something."[15] While I may be able to transmit information to another person (as when I tell someone the number 7 bus goes past my house), and while she may be justified in accepting that information (say, she knows I want her to reach my house), she cannot be said to have been given knowledge. Augustine, like Plato, has special requirements for what can count as knowledge (*scientia*). Knowledge requires the kind of firsthand justification provided by seeing something for oneself, like coming to understand a mathematical proof, as opposed to merely hearing it described by a teacher. Real knowledge—more descriptively called *understanding*—involves having a sense of a whole and seeing all the connections that make something evident. For Burnyeat's Augustine, the truth that illuminates the whole and gives true understanding to our minds is God, present to the mind as the inner teacher, "the one source of understanding."[16] Understanding comes not through words but through seeing for myself, with a mind illuminated by Truth.

On this reading, Christ, the Word, is a cosmic accomplice in ensuring that minds are rightly informed when words are spoken. Because human finitude leaves us unable to use words to teach others, it may appear that God has given us Christ as a deus ex machina who fills in the gaps and guarantees that two minds both contemplate the very same idea. Burnyeat concludes that Wittgenstein selectively quoted Augustine at the opening of the *Philosophical Investigations* to signal to his readers that the *Investigations* takes up Augustine's problem about the complexity of human understanding while leaving aside Augustine's theological solution. Wittgenstein offers an account of understanding not rooted in divine favor and the Platonic mind, but in those rules of agreement that constitute a natural or human explanation for the phenomenon of understanding.[17] Unlike Augustine, Wittgenstein resolves the problem on "naturalistic, purely human terms."[18]

Burnyeat invokes a distinction between theology and naturalism as an explanation, but it fails to explain much. It certainly does not shed light on how to understand *De magistro*.[19] The distinction is less obvious than Burnyeat assumes, and it would be unintelligible to Augustine. What some parse as philosophy and theology exist, unified, in the motivating issues of the dialogue. Some readers have proposed that the so-called theological solution Augustine offers is not so much discreditable as it is not theological, in any Christian sense. One commentator suggests that it might be possible to naturalize Augustine's own theory.[20] That theory can live on in secular garb, "provided that reference to Christ, the Inner Teacher, is stripped of its explicitly theological meaning."[21] Another commentator, Phillip Cary, suggests Augustine's theology fails as adequate theology, perhaps effectively naturalizing itself. In short, Augustine is accused of being too theological, needlessly theological, and not theological enough. The distinction between theology and naturalism fails to hold up, and it fails to make sense of Augustine's dialogue.

Cary argues that Augustine's epistemology and theology are inseparable in *De magistro*. On Cary's account, it looks like the theological and the natural—however we parse those terms—are bound together for Augustine. Cary maintains that Augustine's distinction between sign and signified maps onto the distinction between carnal and spiritual: "for the early Augustine what Plato calls 'intelligible,' the Bible calls 'spiritual.' Indeed sensible/intelligible, carnal/spiritual, outer/inner, and lower/higher are all ways of stating the same fundamental dichotomy."[22] Cary agrees with Burnyeat that the apparent skeptical problem of *De magistro* is motivated by Augustine's Platonic inheritance. In what he terms Augustine's "expressionist semiotics," words—like any sensible thing—give external expression to deeper, more real things. But because words are sensible things, they can never give full expression to what is intelligible and thus can never give true knowledge of things.[23] No external thing like a word or gesture can enable anyone to see truth or know God.

Instead, Cary writes, the education of the soul takes place through inner teaching and is "accomplished directly by God without external means like words, signs and sacraments, or human flesh."[24] We come to know, not through words, but through the teaching of Truth who dwells within. According to Cary, Augustine's portrait of Truth in *De magistro* does not reflect the Pauline notion of Christ dwelling in a heart by faith but rather a Platonist notion of an intellectual vision of what is intelligible.[25] This inner teacher is the "very condition of the possibility of rational knowledge and understanding, and thus of the kind of learning that any good student of the liberal disciplines can accomplish."[26] If the inner teacher serves only to bestow an intellectual vision of intelligible truth, then clearly he has little to do with the incarnation.[27] This teacher may be called Christ, but cannot be identified with Christ the man, Jesus of Nazareth. On Cary's view, Augustine's inward turn is a turn away from the life-giving flesh of Christ, even as it is a turn toward Christ's divinity.[28]

The effect of this expressionist semiotics is to turn Augustine and Adeo-datus away from what is natural, outward, and material. To know God, as to know anything else, one must turn inward and away from what is bodily. This view invites them to turn away from Christ's body, to turn away from frail words, and to turn away from human relationships. Augustine is nei-ther Adeodatus's teacher nor his father—not in the way that really counts.[29] On Cary's view, *De magistro* offers an unsatisfying epistemology, having nothing to do with what is sensible, and an unsatisfying theology, where God is utterly disincarnate and theology is reduced merely to an investi-gation into the conditions of knowledge.[30] Having no real substance of its own, the theological collapses into the natural.

One solution to the apparent failure of words and signs might be a realm of intelligibility where we can learn directly from the things them-selves. Michael Mendelson identifies that realm of intelligibility with what Augustine calls the beata vita. He highlights what he calls *De magistro*'s "eu-daimonistic interlude," a moment midway through the dialogue where Au-gustine tells his son their conversation is preparing the two of them to enter and breathe the air of the blessed life.[31] Mendelson identifies Augustine's "eudaimonistic haven" as an intelligible realm wherein the soul learns truth through an unmediated act of acquaintance with it. The promise of the in-telligible realm is that it allows us to rise above our individual minds and words to reach a reliable and public place where "we can rest in the quiet embrace of a Truth so true it can never fade or disappear."[32] The intelligible realm promises us freedom from our inward isolation and from the pos-sibilities of loss and confusion. Mendelson reads it as Augustine's solution to the anxiety and frustration that dog mortal life and human speaking.

Mendelson finds in the dialogue a path out of heartbreak. He con-ceives of the beata vita as a realm of intelligibility beyond the confines of broken mortal life. For Mendelson, that brokenness cuts deeply: "Embod-ied souls gesturing across an unnavigable kind of distance, language an instrument that must always fall short of the mark, vulnerable souls osten-sibly crippled by immersion and drifting irrevocably towards ostensibly in-evitable loss—this is a grim landscape indeed."[33] Mendelson's vision of the beata vita is a response to grief, both the possibility of losing those one loves but also the more routine possibilities of speaking words that fail to move, fail to illuminate, fail to connect. It is a tempting picture, one promising safety and security. This beata vita comes, however, at the price of renouncing what matters most. Loss was probably on Augustine's mind as he wrote up the dialogue, likely not long after the untimely death of his promising son, his last tie to his partner of many years. Yet it is hard to imagine that the hope of a disembodied realm of intelligibility would provide any comfort to a father's grieving heart.

The problematic framing of the problem leads to problematic solutions. Augustine is accused of solving his skeptical problem by turning to spirit— some kind of theological or divine solution. His apparent conception of spirit fails to satisfy both those who want theology and those who do not. Yet the meaning of spirit is underdetermined in these readings of the dialogue. It is constructed only out of a sense of the inadequacy or unintelligibility of bodies and human speech. If all we can find in this dialogue is a description of a skeptical problem where the differences of body block intelligibility, we will be very bad readers of spirit, inventing dissatisfying forms of divinity. We will end up with an inner teacher who is a cosmically powerful mind-fixer, a disincarnate Truth who leaves souls even more alienated from one another. We will end up with a dialogue stripped of human relationship and meaning. We will end up with a beata vita promising escape from confusion and loss. If we read this dialogue as a solution to a skeptical problem of meaning, we miss its real wisdom.

The word *spirit* is here a label masquerading as an explanation. In a discussion of ostensive teaching in his *Philosophical Investigations*, Ludwig Wittgenstein puzzles over what it means to draw someone's attention specifically to the color or shape of an object. He notes that when we can find no single bodily action we can call "pointing out the shape," we say whatever activity corresponds to those words is *geistige* (i.e., spiritual or mental). He concludes, "Where our language suggests a body and there is none: there, we should like to say, is a *spirit* (*Geist*)."[34] Wittgenstein's point is that the label is no explanation. What is spiritual or divine is, in his example, defined not by any content of its own but simply by its being nonbodily. Spirit is only what is left over after the so-called deficiencies of the body are stripped out. Readers of *De magistro* should hesitate to slap a similarly underdetermined label on the inner teacher and the beata vita.

Much of the scholarship on *De magistro* suggests that Augustine's imagination for spirit comes out of dissatisfaction with the possibilities for the words we share with one another. Such readings give short shrift to the real possibilities of spirit.

I do not share the conviction that Augustine means for readers to find some neat solution (theological, philosophical, or otherwise) to the skeptical problem with which he is supposedly preoccupied. My reading is unusual in questioning whether Augustine really means, in the end, for us to agree with him that we talk only to inform. If we accept Augustine's odd suggestion that talking is all about informing, we embrace what Augustine thinks is a temptation to be resisted.[35] Augustine invites us to *test* his picture of a contracted motivation for language, not accept it whole cloth. We may initially and unreflectively answer the question "What are we trying to accomplish when we speak with one another?" with the response "To inform." But by the end of the dialogue, if we still think talking is only for informing, we have missed Augustine's insight.[36]

Put differently, Augustine is not so superficial that he cannot see the skeptical problem. He sees the skeptical problem as a superficial problem. Though Augustine shows that the meaning of any sign is underdetermined by its use, he does not go on to draw a skeptical conclusion about the communicability of meaning. Augustine acknowledges there are times when he and his son have mistaken each other's meanings, even in quite deep ways. Yet the specter of potential confusion and misapprehension does not lead Augustine to conclude that no communication ever happens. Nor are the ways he and his son miss each other's meanings always a source of pain.

For Augustine, God and creation are bound together in such a way that a turn toward spirit is not a turn away from external things and the created order. Instead, it is a turn toward it, richly conceived. The beata vita is not reached through escaping external things. It is instead a birth into life with others. For Augustine, relating to the inner teacher cannot be divorced from loving his very son, the boy Adeodatus. Likewise, knowing God cannot be divorced from loving God's son, the Word made flesh. Augustine's concern is not to teach his son and us, his readers, to replace our fragile words with an immaterial, divine, transparent, intelligible Word. Instead, he invites us to consider whether we're seeing a problem where there is none. The way words resist our attempts to use them only to inform should cause us to reconsider what we are doing with them at all.

Let us return now to the opening pages of De magistro. Unlike most commentators who readily adopt Augustine's odd suggestion that we use words only to inform, Adeodatus puts up more resistance. While Adeodatus readily agrees to the claim that we ask questions to inform those we question what we want, he needs more persuading that informing is *all* that we attempt to effect when we speak. When Augustine presses, Adeodatus wonders about singing, which involves words but is often done while one is alone and therefore cannot be thought to involve informing someone. Brushing off Augustine's suggestion that we sing for the same reason we talk—to inform or to remind (a way of informing)—Adeodatus asserts that he sings to enjoy (*delectandi*) himself (*mag.* 1.1). Augustine breezily assures his son that the counterexample does not hold up: speaking and singing are quite separable. Either the singer aims to inform others through words, or the singer simply takes enjoyment in the melody and the words are incidental, not functioning as speech. Inasmuch as singing is talking, it does inform. Inasmuch as singing is music, it does not (*mag.* 1.1). Singing apparently cannot stand as a counterexample to the claim that all talking aims at informing.

Adeodatus's passing remark about enjoyment marks one more experience with language occluded by Augustine's (provisional) insistence on a narrow sense of why we talk. The pleasure elicited by the father-son conversation of De magistro with its jokes, puns, and playfulness is foreshadowed by Adeodatus's suggestion that language might sometimes simply be pleasurable, joyous, and even idle. Anyone who has recited a catchy poem or contrived a cunning phrase knows the pleasure and delight we take in language. But here, father persuades son that he takes pleasure not from the words of his songs but rather from the tunes. Pleasure is strangely disavowed as a motivation for speaking, despite the evidence of the ensuing text and of Adeodatus and Augustine's experience.

Adeodatus gives one more objection to the claim that we talk only to inform and remind: prayer. Talking cannot be only for the purpose of informing or reminding, thinks Adeodatus, because prayer is a kind of talking, and it would be impious to suggest that God's creatures could teach or remind him. One scholar writes that the passage raises a "significant puzzle about why we speak in prayer, when we hardly believe that we can teach or remind God of anything."[37] Augustine has a ready answer: the talking involved in prayer is for the sake of the edification of the faithful, not for the purpose of informing God. "Therefore, speaking—saying words aloud—is not needed for praying, unless it is done like priests do, giving signs drawn from memory, not so that God would hear, but that men would and so be raised to God through their shared remembrance."[38] When Christ, "the highest teacher of all," taught the faithful to pray using specific words (as in the *Pater Noster*), he was teaching them not the words but the things signified by words. When we pray silently or otherwise appear to talk to ourselves, we are simply remembering—calling to mind—the things signified by the words. Accordingly, Augustine argues, we use words in prayer either to inform other minds or our own mind, but not to inform God. In prayer, we talk to God not by means of articulate noise (*articulatum sonum*), but through a wordless call from the hidden part of the rational soul—a hidden part that is called the inner man (*homo interior*) (*mag.* 1.2). This inner call needs no exterior expression because God already knows what we most need. God has perfect access to our interior life. Indeed, in the form of the Holy Spirit he dwells within us. Therefore there is no need to translate inner life into articulated sounds in order to be known by God.

This is a strange account of prayer. It is perhaps a comforting thought to imagine a deity so attuned to my needs that they need no expression on my part. I can imagine such a relationship by limited analogy with my husband's attunement to my needs. He often knows before I do when I need an hour at the piano or a dinner out or an interruption of some self-deprecating narrative. In my relationship with my husband, I need not always express my needs before I am given good things. On the other hand, it is odd to imagine a relationship where, once someone knew my needs, there would be nothing more to say—no joke-telling or reminiscing, no encouraging, nor any other noninforming sharing of words. But that is precisely what Augustine describes: a relationship where God has such an intimate knowledge of me that there is no real point in my directing words to heaven. Such words might inform me or my hearers—but they could say nothing to God. Such a relationship sounds stilted and awkward at best, stunted and dying at worst.

Already within the first few pages of the dialogue, Augustine's thesis that we talk to inform has committed him to surprising conclusions. Large swathes of ordinary human experience of language have been discarded: speaking for pleasure or to figure out what to say or to grow in intimacy. Augustine affects to maintain that these are not real motivations for speaking, nor constitutive features of language. Dismissing all counterexamples to his thesis, Augustine leads his son further and further away from his natural understanding of speaking.

Augustine's comments on prayer, strange as they are, hint at the later insight of the dialogue. At this point in the dialogue, Augustine insists that prayer and talking are totally dissimilar. Indeed he must hold this view, given the thesis he is defending. If speaking serves only to inform, prayer cannot be a form of speaking. God needs no informing. If prayer is a form of speaking, it is a way of talking only to myself or to others.[39] Augustine doubles down on the claim that prayer and talking are totally dissimilar.

Yet while the dialogue opens with a sharp division between prayer and speech, it ends by drawing the two back together. Augustine ultimately concludes that we speak with one another to help each other hear the voice of Christ, the inner teacher. Speaking and prayer are bound together, as we will come to see. Augustine is right that prayer is not a matter of informing. This is true not because God is omniscient (though God is) but because any relationship where conversations aim only at informing is pathological. We cannot escape informing, however, simply by not using words. As another commentator puts it, "How is a wordless inner petition any less of an attempt to inform God than the chatty variety?"[40] Indeed, it may not be. Our preoccupation with getting God to understand what we mean may distract us from the more fundamental question: do we seek intimacy with God?

Augustine's metaphor for prayer in *De magistro* is the *cubiculum*.[41] Prayer takes place in *clausus cubiculis*, in the enclosed bedrooms—which is to say, Augustine explains, in the deep recesses of the soul, the bedrooms of the heart (*mag.* 1.2). In late antiquity, a *cubiculum* was traditionally a multifunctional space used for private and personal activities like sexual activity, rest, and study, but also for hosting important business meetings and honored guests.[42] While Latin writers commonly depicted the *cubiculum* as a secret place, where immoral or indiscreet acts could be committed, a parallel convention associates the *cubiculum* with more laudable activities such as philosophical study and writing. In those activities, secrecy is sought not as cover for bad behavior but as shield from distraction and interruption. While many Christian late antique writers worried about the dangers of the pagan or heretical activities that might take place within the *cubiculum*, some Christian authors "emphasized the space's central place within the household's moral topography by describing it as a site of radical seclusion from worldly influences, and as the place where one would most likely encounter the divine."[43] Drawing on passages like Matthew 6 ("When you pray, go into your *cubiculum*, shut the door, pray to your Father who is in secret"), Christian writers adopted the *cubiculum* as an image of the place where God and the soul could commune. "While still very much a room associated with secrecy, solitude, and self-improvement, the *cubiculum* became synonymous in late antiquity with an intense experience of spiritual intimacy, as the place where one performed and potentially experienced his or her relationship to God."[44] Christian authors likened the space of the *cubiculum* to the heart or soul, "and thus to the presence of the divine within the individual."[45]

For Augustine, prayer turns out to be a matter not of informing but of intimacy. The bedroom of the heart, a space both private and shared, is a place of spiritual intimacy, where God and the soul dwell together. The soul does not enter the bedrooms of the heart looking simply for satisfaction of its own desire. What draws the soul there is a desire to be with God, a desire to be where God is. It is a place where God and the soul attend to one another. Prayer in the bedroom with God is not good because it is wordless and not mixed up with external things. It is wordless because it is so good, and the soul needs no more reminders, no more signs to focus its attention.

Prayer is not a matter of informing, but a matter of intimacy. Augustine says nothing like this—he says very nearly the opposite—but his image suggests it. This moment is the first of several in *De magistro* where Augustine's explicit views are in strange tension with the passage or images he explores. As I detail in subsequent chapters, Augustine sets up this tension for good pedagogical reasons. At this point, however, we need only notice the tension between Augustine's stated view that prayer is only for informing and his evocative image of prayer in the heart's bedroom. This intimate image of a shared inner space is the text's first hint that ordinary speaking might turn out to have something to do with intimacy too.

The assumption that we try (and fail) to use words only to inform leads to strange interpretive consequences. When we assume that Augustine's theological or spiritual insights are solutions to epistemological problems, we misunderstand those insights, shoehorning them into a bad fit. These so-called solutions set intimacy and intelligibility at odds, making the inner teacher into a powerful mind-fixer and the beata vita into an escape from human life. Such readings neglect the impact of Augustine's initial question, with its attention to human desire and connection. *What do we want to accomplish when we speak with one another?* In the second half of this book, I argue that *De magistro* demonstrates that speaking is not all about informing. The next two chapters, however, explore the strange forms of life engendered by the conviction that we talk only to inform. Augustine's odd comments about prayer are only the beginning of the strangeness. Wittgenstein is surely right when he says that "to imagine a language means to imagine a form of life."[46] In the first part of *De magistro*, Augustine invites Adeodatus and us to imagine a form of life: how do we live when we suppose being in touch with *logos* is only a matter of informing and being informed?

CHAPTER TWO

PRELUDE

If Augustine does not want his son to believe we talk only to inform, why is he so insistent on the point in the opening pages of *De magistro*? Why does he spend so much of the dialogue exploring how words signify meanings to minds? Why do father and son create a detailed taxonomy of *words that designate other signs* and *words that designate things*, when in the end all words are simply names for meanings? Why does Augustine press his son to agree to such a narrowed account of language, when that account will be discarded by the end of the dialogue?

Augustine's views about language in the first half of the dialogue comprise a series of contractions. The scope of what words do (and of what we can do with words) becomes narrower and narrower as the conversation unfolds. *We talk to inform and be informed* becomes *We talk only to inform*. *Words teach by signifying realities to minds* becomes *Words cannot teach at all*. *Words are many parts of speech* becomes *All words are nouns/names*. Instead of reminding us of the great variety of things we do with words, Augustine, himself a master of words, seems to limit the power and scope of what we can do with them.

Yet my description of the dialogue as a series of propositions and counterpropositions is misleading. It hides the back-and-forth of the conversation. It makes tidy what is untidy. As Augustine and Adeodatus try to explain how words inform, it is hardly smooth sailing. There are false starts, confusion, and dropped threads. Views are overturned. There are moments of conversational breakdown. Indeed, there is a strange tension between, on the one hand, the apparent commitment to the thesis that we talk to inform and, on the other hand, the provisional way the conversation unfolds. The thesis that we talk to inform hardly receives an airtight defense.

However illuminating Augustine's and Adeodatus's parsing of signs may be, their activity, when abstracted from the intimate relationship they share, reveals blind spots as well. This chapter takes up two key moments of breakdown resulting from the contracted view of language that Augustine and Adeodatus consider. The first moment is Augustine and Adeodatus's attempt to say what is signified by each word in a line of Virgilian poetry. The exercise falls apart halfway through the line, and their efforts to clarify how words signify seem to lead them to neglect the ways words are bound up with and take their meaning from life. The second moment of breakdown is Adeodatus's confusion about how to answer his father's question whether he is *homo*. Flustered, Adeodatus proposes setting up a rule to limit the ambiguity of words—and in this way, he seems to suggest that precision and clarity make language communicative. In these moments, I will argue, Augustine's careful orchestration of the text shows us how much is lost when we suppose we talk to inform, using words to sign our meanings.

Augustine calls this part of the conversation a set of exercises (*mag.* 8.21). This description may explain why Augustine is willing to drop threads, equivocate, and otherwise fail to take the argument as seriously as we might expect. These exercises are clever and interesting, but preparatory. So what is the point of these strange contractions? What is the exercise preparatory to? A careful examination of these moments of breakdown will lay the groundwork for answers to those questions.

Having agreed that they talk to inform, Augustine and Adeodatus turn to an investigation of how words inform the minds of interlocutors. They agree that words are signs (*uerba signa esse*), and since a sign cannot be a sign without signifying anything, they agree that a word must signify something (*mag.* 2.3). When we utter words, we do not make sounds for no reason. As Adeodatus reminds his father, we speak to help each other understand something (*mag.* 2.3). Words signify realities, and we utter words to point the mind of an interlocutor toward the reality we have in mind.

To illustrate his point, Augustine invites Adeodatus to consider a line from Virgil: "si nihil ex tanta superis placet urbe relinqui" (*mag.* 2.3).

Adeodatus notes that there are eight words and thus eight signs.[1] He says he understands the line of verse very well, but when Augustine invites him to explain what each word signifies (*quid singula uerba significent*), it is far from easy. Taking the first word, Adeodatus says he sees what *if* (*si*) signifies, but he cannot give another word to explain it. Prompted by his father, he proposes that *if* signifies doubt in the mind, and he quickly moves on. For the next word, *nothing* (*nihil*), Adeodatus has a ready account: "What does *nothing* signify if not what doesn't exist?"[2] Augustine, however, is doubtful: "Maybe you're right, but I'm hesitant to agree. You admitted earlier that a sign can't be a sign without signifying something. What doesn't exist certainly can't be something. Therefore, the second word in this line, since it doesn't signify something, is not a sign. And we were wrong to agree that all words are signs or that every sign signifies something."[3] Adeodatus is unpersuaded, and he expresses confidence not merely in the abstract principle but in the person of his father:

> You're pushing too hard. It would be very silly for us to utter a word without meaning to signify anything. As you talk with me now, I am sure no sound you make is pointless. All your utterances are so many signs, offered to help me understand something. So you shouldn't utter those two syllables [no-thing] while we're talking, if you don't mean to signify anything by them. If, however, you realize you need those syllables to make some utterance—one that informs or reminds us of something when we hear it—then surely you realize too what I mean to say, even though I can't explain it.[4]

Augustine offers that *nothing*—like *if*—might signify a state of mind rather than a thing, and Adeodatus readily agrees. Augustine then proposes they move on lest they suffer the absurdity of being held up by *nothing*. "Pretty funny, all right,"[5] comments Adeodatus. It is easy to imagine father and son sharing a laugh over their predicament. After that, they are not able to get much further in the exercise. Adeodatus takes up the third word, *from* (*ex*), and offers the synonym *out of.* Augustine is dissatisfied with the response, saying he is looking for the thing signified, not just another word. At this point, the Virgilian exercise is abandoned, and the two move on to a consideration of ostensive definition and its limits.

The point of the Virgilian exercise is to examine how words signify. On those terms, it fails.[6] Adeodatus is unable to explain what is signified by each of the words *si, nihil, ex.* (The exercise ends right before the one word—*urbe*—Adeodatus might have been able to handle, by pointing to or otherwise showing a city.) But if the exercise fails in an obvious way, it fails in another, more subtle way, too. Or perhaps failure is the wrong category. The quoted line is a place where meaning flares out, beyond the limits of the exercise they have set for themselves. The line of poetry resists and contradicts the account of language Augustine and Adeodatus are defending. As such, it is a teaching moment, showing the limits of the account and reminding them of the richness of meanings in the words they share.

Father and son make no mention of the original context of the line, but they knew it well. The line is taken from the end of the second book of Virgil's *Aeneid*, where, at Dido's insistence, Aeneas retells the story of the destruction of Troy. Even though his "heart shrinks back / From memory,"[7] Aeneas tells of the Greeks' trick, the blindness of the Trojans, and the scenes of devastation. He describes Trojan Priam who witnesses the impious slaughter of Polites, his son, at the hands of Greek Pyrrhus. Aeneas describes how his mother, Venus, restrains his murderous rage and reminds him of his obligation to return to his father, Anchises; his son, little Iulus; and his wife, Creusa.

Finding Anchises in their ancestral home, Aeneas tries to take his father into the mountains to safety. Anchises, however, is resolved to die in the city, within the walls of his home. The tears and pleading of the whole household—Aeneas, Iulus, Creusa, and others—cannot change his mind. Pious Aeneas cannot abandon his father to the enemy. He begs,

> If out of towering Troy the gods leave nothing,
> If you're resolved to give this dying city
> Yourself and us, the door to that stands open—
> To Pyrrhus, soaked with Priam's blood, who kills
> The son and then the father at the altar.
> Sweet mother, did you save me from the flames
> Of war for this? The enemy in my home,
> My son, my father, and Creusa lying
> Streaked in each other's blood, like slaughtered cattle?[8]

Aeneas does not speak simply to inform, to make his father think of certain realities: the danger of the city, the safety of the mountains. Instead, his poignant speech urges his father to imagine what his stubbornness will produce: the indignity of the Greek penetration of their ancestral home, the impossibility of protecting Troy from the deities bent on destroying it, the impiety of failing to protect his family.

When Aeneas's desperate words fail to move his father, he takes up his sword and shield to return to battle. Yet Creusa, standing on the threshold, holds out Iulus before him, asking, "To whom do you leave Iulus, / Your father, and me—your wife but soon your widow?"[9] As if in response, an "amazing portent" appears, and flames, vivid but harmless, lick the head of Iulus. The sign of divine favor is confirmed by the sudden appearance of a comet in the sky. These signs promise a bright future for his grandson and family, and they are, finally, what move Anchises to leave the city with his family. Aeneas lifts his father onto his shoulders and takes the little fingers of Iulus in his hand, as Creusa walks behind the other three. With his family by his side, Aeneas is frightened by every noise, and at the sight of his Greek enemies, he takes fearful flight. Discovering that he has outrun Creusa, Aeneas races back through the city, vainly searching for his lost wife.

When Augustine asks Adeodatus to explain what each of Virgil's eight words signifies, they approach the passage with a level of abstraction that belies their grammatical and literary educations. They intentionally contract the scope of meaning as they try to capture the reality signified by each word. Yet meaning swells out between them, in a way that challenges their attempts to get a determinate fix on the meaning of each word. Each word signifies slightly differently, according to the context in which it is spoken. At least four contexts are relevant: the context of the invented conversation between Aeneas and Anchises, the context of the invented conversation between Aeneas and Dido, the context of Virgil and his Roman readers, and the context of the conversation between Augustine and Adeodatus. In none of these cases can we say that each word in the line signifies some single reality.

Let us begin with the narrowest frame: Aeneas to Anchises. Aeneas's words acknowledge the greatness of the city Anchises loves, even as he reminds Anchises that the gods are hell-bent on destroying it. Adeodatus says that *if* (*si*) signifies "doubt in the mind," but that is a thin explanation for the word as used here. *If* sets up a subjunctive, describing the bloody consequences that will follow from Anchises's stubborn insistence on remaining in the city fated for destruction. The second word is even more full of meaning than Adeodatus's explanation lets on. The *nothing* described in the line is, of course, not the absolute nothingness over which Augustine and Adeodatus stumble, but the nothingness left by the devastation of war: bloodied bodies, abandoned and ransacked homes, desecrated altars, free men turned slaves. The *nothing* to which the gods will soon reduce Troy is no confusing abstraction, but a scene of immeasurable loss. When Aeneas speaks these words, he does not signify determinate realities. He gestures, frantically and hyperbolically, beyond the limits of his knowledge and the powers of his expression.

Within the context of the *Aeneid*, Aeneas speaks those words aloud not to his father but to Dido. The words are reported speech, as he tells Dido and her household the story of the fall of Troy. Dido has a different set of contexts and concerns than does Aeneas. The realities signified by those eight words are hardly the same in any case. Dido, having loved and lost, and now falling in love with Aeneas, heard them differently than did Anchises. A similar point could be made about Virgil, if we move the frame out another level. What did Virgil mean by "ex tanta superis . . . urbe"? What did Aeneas, founder of Rome? How did Anchises understand the statement that the destruction of Troy pleased (*placet*) the gods? How did Virgil understand the claim? Answers to those questions would complicate the straightforward picture of signification on offer.

If we widen the frame one last time, Augustine and Adeodatus appear on the scene. One father-son pair discusses a conversation between another father-son pair. They hear the words of Aeneas, spoken to Anchises, reported to Dido, and invented by Virgil. One scholar suggests that the mention of the destruction of Troy may be something of a metaphor for the account of language that is about to be demolished.[10] Certainly we readers can understand the words in that way. More significantly, though, they conjure ghosts and dreams from the lives of Augustine and Adeodatus. As readers of the *Confessiones* know well, Augustine styles himself throughout that book as Aeneas. At this moment of *De magistro*, Augustine makes a similar move. Augustine does not pick the line out of thin air. Anyone familiar with the epic, including Augustine and Adeodatus, would know full well the story surrounding that line and the parallels between that story and Augustine's own life.

The quoted line evokes familial forms of love that play out in parallel ways in the lives of Aeneas and Augustine.[11] Adeodatus, like little Iulus, is God-beloved, and the bright promise of the boy gives joy to his family. That promise lays a burden of responsibility on Augustine, just as it did for Aeneas. When the sad ghost of Creusa appears to Aeneas, she tells him her death was fated by the gods, and she prophesies that he will have a bright future with a prosperous kingdom and a royal wife. She asks only one thing of Aeneas: "Cherish the child that we created." Aeneas is unable to respond before she disappears. "She left me, cutting short my words and weeping— / I had so much to say—and faded off."[12] Augustine too, having sent away his partner to satisfy his ambition, is left with his empty words, words powerless to secure what he most wants. Like Aeneas, Augustine has only one remaining tether to the woman he loves: his son. His faithfulness to that child is his last form of faithfulness to her. All this is known to both Augustine and Adeodatus, and love and regret lie unspoken between father and son as they determinedly work to nail down the meanings of the words. Perhaps their willingness to abandon the exercise should not surprise us. An ocean of meaning swells between them. It is easier to focus on words and things. When he tells his story to Dido, Aeneas frames his recollection as words of grief. The words are no less so for Augustine and Adeodatus.

I want to be clear: Augustine is not stupid. The failure of the Virgilian exercise is no surprise to him. The unraveling of the view (i.e., that words inform) is no surprise either. This moment of play—of entertaining and exploring what ultimately turns out to be a dead end—is preparatory, as we will see. Augustine and Adeodatus's conversation reveals, to the literate reader, a tension between the straightforward attempt to fix signs to things and the complexity of meaning that swells out and complicates that attempt. There is a lesson in the failure, but that lesson is not a piece of teaching that can be placed into the mind of another. It is a lesson that Augustine and Adeodatus's shared life reveals, if they are able to notice. Words signify realities, to be sure. But when we separate words from life, we speak words that spin ineffectually above the depths of what we most want to say. What is the will of the gods? What is the nothingness of loss they give us?

What words will touch those we love? What do we want in speaking with one another? Augustine and Adeodatus are not without answers to those questions. But those answers play across the boundaries of their failed exercise to explain how words signify determinate realities to minds.

When Adeodatus struggles to define the words of the line for Virgil, Augustine presses his son not to offer mere synonyms. Augustine claims to want not more words or signs, but the reality signified by these signs. At this, Adeodatus balks. He tells his father that he cannot give him the reality sought if their conversation takes place in words. If Augustine wants answers without words, Adeodatus says, he should ask questions without words (*mag.* 3.5). Yet Adeodatus finds he has spoken too soon. Some things *can* be demonstrated without words. We could use bodily actions (rather than words) as signs to demonstrate something to an observer; we could point out a wall, for example, or point to any visible thing. In such cases, the meaning could be clear without any speech (*mag.* 3.5). (Pointing would not be a solution for the difficult words *if*, *nothing*, and *from*, but the point goes unremarked.) Even if we can answer questions and demonstrate things without using the signs of words, it seems we still need to rely on signs of pointing and showing. This conviction falls by the wayside, however, when Augustine and Adeodatus realize it is even possible to demonstrate something without using signs of any sort. In response to a question, we might simply perform the action itself without using signs. For example, if someone asks me what walking is, I can show him by standing up and walking around the room. Answering a question with an appropriate action is a way of answering without signs, unless I am already doing that action I am asked to show.

At this point, Augustine summarizes the tripartite distinction that has emerged in the conversation: signs that represent other signs, signs that signify things (that are not signs), and things that can be demonstrated without signs. An example of the first category was given when Adeodatus offered one sign (*from*) for another (*of*). An example of the second category was given when Augustine talked about pointing (giving a sign) to indicate a thing (a particular wall). And an example of the third category was given when Augustine explained that we could respond to a question about what an action was by doing that action. The first category—signs that signify other signs—occupies father and son for the next several pages until they arrive at the curious conclusion that every word is a noun or name (*nomen*). The thesis that every word is a noun/name lays the groundwork for the second moment of breakdown, as we will see. It is also part of the contraction of language into which Augustine draws his son in the first part of the dialogue. In arguing that every word is a *nomen*, Augustine is once again drawing his son into a claim that at first blush seems odd (*mag.* 4.9).[13] Both father and son have had sufficient grammatical education to know the distinction between a noun (*nomen*) and a word (*uerbum*). *Nomen* (which can be translated into English as either *noun* or *name*) is a sign of other signs, and it is also itself a *uerbum*. The word *nomen* signifies other words like *grapefruit* and *brioche*, while also itself being word. According to basic grammar, though, not every *uerbum* is a *nomen*. Some words are other parts of speech like adjectives or adverbs. *Uerbum* is to *nomen*, Augustine suggests, as animal is to horse. All horses are animals but not all animals are horses, just as each *uerbum* is a *nomen*, but not every *nomen* is a *uerbum*.

Yet the horse analogy breaks down in this way: *nomen* and *uerbum* are words that mutually signify, but the words *horse* and *animal* do not. When the two use the terms *word* and *noun*, they are using two words and they are also using two nouns. Therefore, Augustine wonders aloud how the two terms differ, apart from their spelling and punctuation. The dialogue began with the ready assumption that two terms (*docere* and *discere*) were quite different, before one was shown to be reducible to the other: Augustine and Adeodatus now face the surprising upset of another ostensibly straightforward claim: that *nomen* and *uerbum* each signify a different *res*. Augustine now maintains that every *uerbum* is a *nomen*.

Augustine offers Adeodatus several justifications for the claim. First, Augustine points out that a pronoun—which takes the place of a noun—can be used to refer to a group of conjunctions (*and, moreover, but, yet* [*mag.* 5.13]). That is, we could refer to that group of words within a sentence with a term like *those*, a pronoun that takes the place of a noun. When Adeodatus, balking at the implication that conjunctions are nouns, suggests that *those* implies *those words*, Augustine tries a second tack, an analysis of St. Paul's statement that "With Christ there is no Is and is not, only an Is." Augustine maintains this is equivalent to saying (*mag.* 5.14), "What is called an Is is with Christ," which statement is itself equivalent to saying, "What is named an Is is with Christ." Though one would ordinarily say that *is* is a verb, in this case *Is* is a noun because it names Christ. Indeed, explains Augustine, this logic can be extended to all parts of speech, each of which can function as names/nouns, and he leaves it to Adeodatus to follow out the argument later. By way of a third demonstration of the claim, Augustine, reminding his son that each sentence is composed of a noun and a verb, shows that a variety of terms (including conjunctions) can function as nouns (*mag.* 5.16). For example, someone teaching a small child how to ask permission might say something like, "*May* is correct, but *Can* is wrong." *May* and *Can* would ordinarily be identified as verbs, but in such a situation they clearly function as nouns. Considering the matter settled, Augustine and Adeodatus move on, noting that *nomen* and *uocabulum* overlap each other, and that *nomen* and the Greek *onoma* differ only by their sound and thus are signs that signify themselves and each other.

Before we follow Augustine and Adeodatus forward in the dialogue to a respite from these careful distinctions, we should pause over this curious line of argumentation. Why is Augustine so keen to demonstrate that every word is a noun/name? And why does he not clarify that the entire discussion turns on a pun on the word *nomen*, which in Latin, as in English, can mean both *name* and *noun*? Certainly he does not mean to suggest that the distinctions made by grammarians among the parts of speech are unnecessary or nonsensical. The claim that all words are names does not mean that every word serves the grammatical function of a noun. Augustine the rhetorician would not make such a basic mistake. Rather, he is noting that any word, no matter what part of speech it is, is a name for a meaning. In making this argument, Augustine here seems to side with the Stoics, who held that every word signifies something, as against Plutarch and the Peripatetics, who held that only nouns and verbs signify, while other words are at best "co-significant."[14] One scholar links Augustine's thesis that every word is a name with the Stoic Chrysippus's famous dictum that "every word is by nature ambiguous."[15] Every word is ambiguous, in that every word can signify both a thing and itself (qua word). Even words that do not signify something visible still signify something, and they can still be said to be signs. All words are names inasmuch as they signify some relatively stable meaning.[16] According to the Stoic doctrine of autonymy, a single term can both signify itself and signify an extralinguistic object. That is to say, it can name itself and name another object, which is why it is possible to talk about words themselves, in addition to using them to talk about extralinguistic objects. This early version of the use-mention distinction was little noticed in late antiquity: "Today only Augustine can be seen to have appreciated and deliberately exploited its usefulness."[17]

Yet the claim that all words are names is not just an ancient dispute for Augustine. It is also part of the preparatory exercise, laying the groundwork for what is to come. We sometimes act as though this picture is an accurate image of how language functions, and this misapprehension is worth our attention. Reducing all words to names for meanings gives us the illusion of a control over our words, and this apparent mastery facilitates an exchange of information with another. When I think of a word as a name for a meaning, I have a grasp on what I am trying to communicate. The meaning named by a word is something stable and static even though the named thing itself may disappear or change—as a family table could be burned up but still be talked about.[18] Ordinarily my grasp seems to extend to the mind of my interlocutor. That is to say, usually the connection between a word and what it names seems quite secure, and I use it to teach my interlocutor about what I mean. The stability of meaning seems like it increases the utility of words. A thing is unambiguously captured by its name and can thus be communicated without ambiguity (which it could not if, say, one were speaking playfully or poetically). The meaning of the word I speak is under my control, and I can pass it along to another mind. The meaning named is something specific and determinate—or at least that is the hope—and so I can speak out of the confidence of having a fix on meanings, a fix that might even extend my control to the mind of the one with whom I speak. Yet to think of words in this way is to oversimplify, as Augustine well knows. It locates meaning in the wrong place, in the stability of words, rather than in the human connection and understanding that make words meaningful.[19]

Augustine illustrates this richer picture of language in the next section of the conversation, an amusing exchange about whether Adeodatus is a human being (*homo*). This part of the dialogue illustrates the utility of the use-mention distinction, but performs the more important function of reminding Adeodatus and us about the intimacy that motivates our speaking together. Augustine begins by asking Adeodatus "utrum homo homo sit" (whether man is man).[20] Adeodatus is perplexed by the question, so Augustine asks whether the two syllables *ho* and *mo* taken together mean *homo* (man). When Adeodatus agrees about the meaning, Augustine then asks whether Adeodatus himself is those two syllables, *ho* and *mo*. Having admitted that he is not identical with the two syllables *ho* and *mo*, but unwilling to accept the conclusion that he is not a man, Adeodatus is flustered. His words—and his father's words—suddenly seem to have become unreliable tools for informing. When he says he is not *man*, he wants to be understood in one way (as not identical with the sounds of the syllables) and not another (as not identical with a living human person) (*mag.* 8.22).

Adeodatus protests he cannot answer the question unless he knows whether Augustine is asking whether he, Adeodatus, is the two syllables (*duabus istis syllabis*) or the thing signified by the two syllables (*re ipsa quam significant*). Augustine observes that Adeodatus has taken the word *homo* in two senses (as an articulated sound and as a sign of some referent), but has treated all the other words in the sentence as instances of the latter. (To be fair, Augustine led him to do so by the series of questions he asked.) In response, Adeodatus announces that he will now take the word the same as all the other words, as signifying a referent, and he proposes a rule that words should always be taken as referring to their referents. This is, in effect, an attempt (unwitting or no) to reject the Stoic doctrine of autonomy, to reject mention and opt for use alone.

Augustine is skeptical about Adeodatus's rule. He reminds Adeodatus of the joker who asked his interlocutor whether what someone says comes out of his mouth (as opposed to some other part of his body). When the unsuspecting interlocutor agreed to the principle, the joker made him say the word *lion* and then claimed that a lion had come out of the interlocutor's mouth. If we only treat signs in terms of the things to which they refer, Augustine asks, how could we escape the joke's conclusion? Adeodatus, finally seeing the utility of the distinction between sign and referent (or between phonetic and semantic content), admits that the signified thing does not come out of the speaker's mouth—only the sign does. The distinction turns out to be useful after all. If Augustine asks whether *homo* is a noun, the answer is yes, because the question clearly pertains to the sign itself. But if Augustine asks whether Adeodatus is *homo*, the answer is also yes, because the mind inclines to what is signified. Father and son agree that context can clarify whether the question pertains to the sign or the referent.

It is, finally, the playfulness of the exchange that conveys the real point. Adeodatus wants to set up a rule to secure clarity. He wants to be sure he will be understood, not humiliated. Augustine reminds his son, however, that understanding rests not in the perfection of words and rules of language but in the context of the speaking persons. The failure of words to inform without ambiguity is not a failure of conversation. The real failure comes when we forget that we speak to another human being. Without that acknowledgment, we have, not communication, but a pastiche of more or less meaningless labels for meanings.[21] Adeodatus's confidence in his father allows him to press forward through the confusing territory of the use-mention distinction and come to understand why his father asks the questions he does. There is no way to guarantee that words will inform the mind of another with perfect precision and clarity. There is always the possibility of embarrassment, confusion, or misapprehension. Learning this truth in the context of a loving relationship makes the vulnerability bearable.

Augustine and Adeodatus cover a lot of territory over the course of these pages, but it is tough to say what has been accomplished, given all the dropped threads and discarded lines of argument. Is there some point to the dialectic? Where it is going? Augustine himself raises this question. Immediately after he demonstrates that all words are names, he admits that Adeodatus may wonder what the point of their conversation is:

But with all these detours, it is difficult to say, at this point, where we are headed. Perhaps you think we are just amusing ourselves, diverting our minds from serious matters with schoolboy quibbles; maybe you think we seek some insignificant or trivial end. Or, if you suspect our discussion is giving birth [*parturire*] to something weighty, you want to understand it—or at least to hear what it is. I hope you trust I didn't start this conversation for cheap entertainment. Though we may be playing around, our conversation shouldn't be taken in a trivial sense; we're considering no small or trifling goods. But if I said there is a happy and eternal life to which I hope God—our guide, who is truth itself—might lead us in stages accommodated to our uncertain steps, then I'm afraid I might seem ridiculous, because I started off with a consideration not of the things signified, but of signs. Forgive me, then, this playful prelude. It's not for the sake of mere amusement, but to exercise our mental strength and attention, to prepare us not just to withstand but to love the warmth and light of that place where the happy life is found.[22]

Augustine tells his son to think of their conversation as a playful prelude. In the dialogue, the playfulness of the interaction is revealed not just in the jokes and laughter but also in the fact that the two men are engaged in an interaction not dominated by ends. Together they try out possibilities, figuring out what works and what falls apart. They find themselves at dead ends and confusions. Their words hardly serve as straightforward tools for informing each other. Yet these moments of breakdown prompt not frustration but teasing and laughter. The two speak not out of desperation, trying to make contact, one mind to another. At this part of the conversation, their conclusions are not the point. Instead this prelude—their preplay—reminds them of the ways they speak from their connection with each other. Like all play, theirs is a form of intimacy.

Augustine and Adeodatus's playful prelude serves as interpretative key to the dialogue, unlocking the inner logic of the text. If Augustine wants to release his son and himself from the desire to talk to inform, play is the best possible pedagogy. If the problem is the desire to speak to inform, a didactic presentation of an alternative view is hardly a solution. Play deconstructs the desire to inform, not just by putting more content in the minds of Augustine and Adeodatus, but by reminding them of the intimacy that already undergirds their speaking together. Their playful prelude reminds each of the real way they speak with one another. It also reminds them that their life is the matrix from which meaning is birthed. Their play, therefore, prepares them for what is to come. It will allow them to encounter the beata vita and Christ, the inner teacher, not as solutions to a skeptical problem, but as reminders of connection and invitations to greater attentiveness. Augustine, teacher as he is, knows that they cannot simply drop a problematic view of language and replace it with a correct one. Christ's inner teaching is not simply a piece of teaching that can be passed along.

It is a life into which father and son are invited. Their play prepares them, heart, mind and soul, to desire and love that life.

Alongside the metaphor of play, Augustine offers the metaphor of exercise, saying the conversation serves to exercise their minds and their attention. The metaphor suggests their conversation—or at least this part of it—is preparatory. However clever and interesting it might be, however much the conclusions stand or fall, the conversation is meant to draw them toward something of ultimate significance. Augustine promises that their conversational calisthenics are preparing them not for knowing what words do, but for knowing and loving the blessed life. Their conversation about words and meanings is a spiritual exercise that aims at birthing father and son into the blessed life.

Like ordinary births, it is preceded by a series of contractions. The contractions of language and meaning we have seen in this chapter serve to help Augustine, his son, and his reader to work through a series of related temptations. It is tempting to want to speak to inform the minds of others in a maximally effective way. It is tempting to think my words are what secures my connection with another. It is tempting to forget how much words are bound up with life. It is tempting to think it is the clarity and precision of language that make it communicative. All these temptations are rooted in a fear of vulnerability, a fear of looking foolish, a fear of misunderstanding. Perhaps they are rooted too in a fear of loss. Yet they are also rooted in a strange forgetfulness about our real life with language and with each other. The contraction of language and meaning artificially introduced by Augustine reveals a misguided impulse and, in revealing it, perhaps prepares us to move beyond it. Augustine's curious contraction of words aims not to demolish Adeodatus's natural intuitions about language but instead to draw him into life with God. Through his playful prelude, Augustine draws his son and us, his readers, toward an insight of much deeper significance: we speak not to inform, but to help deliver each other into the beata vita. The following chapter examines how we might imagine, for better or for worse, the divine life toward which our speaking draws us.

CHAPTER THREE

GODS

As we have just seen, Augustine pauses midway through *De magistro* to re-assure Adeodatus that their conversation is not pointless play but aims at matters of real significance. Perhaps a similar assurance is also due in this present book. Augustine has been exploring the temptation to think that we talk primarily to inform, and we might think that some of the issues he has taken up are nitpicky, of interest only to specialists. Yet the problem Augustine describes is neither idiosyncratic nor insignificant. Augustine and Adeodatus's conversation about words taps into something deep, connected to larger issues about how we conceive beatitude, communication, the value of incarnate life, and the relationship between gods and human beings.

Because so much of the interpretation of *De magistro* is shaped by modern concerns about skepticism and clarity, overlooking its deeper significance is easy. We turn now to an unlikely but strategic ally as we try to recover the richness of the text: Luce Irigaray's mythic meditation in *Marine Lover*. While her text makes no explicit reference to Augustine's own, *Marine Lover* helps us examine how we conceive of the relationship between the divine and the human, as well as how we imagine language in relation to the Christian myth. Irigaray is keenly attuned to bad idols of communication, as well as bad simulacra of intimacy, and she serves as an imaginative ally in helping us rescue Augustine's *De magistro* from disincarnate readings.

We have just encountered Augustine's metaphor of birth, which echoes through Irigaray's retelling of the stories of the births of Dionysus, Apollo, and Christ in the final third of *Marine Lover*. In retelling these stories, Irigaray highlights the specifically patriarchal valence of the desire to use words to inform, and she invites her readers to remember how much our speaking is grounded not in control and distance but in intimacy and connection. Augustine does not write about the births of Dionysus and Apollo in *De magistro*, nor does he explicitly invoke Christ's incarnation. Yet Irigaray's retelling of these nativities echoes Augustine's insights about the way that language engenders connection (or fails to), and she is, like him, an unsparing critic of the desire to speak only to inform.

My motivation for turning to Irigaray in this chapter is twofold. First, she highlights the ambivalence about incarnation within certain philosophical and Christian traditions. The stories of the births of Dionysus, Apollo, and Christ present problematic, disincarnate ideals for language. The temptation to talk to inform is tied up with bad ideals of eternity, both pagan and Christian. Irigaray's descriptions of Dionysus and Apollo map onto several disincarnate readings of Christ, the inner teacher of *De magistro*. Like Augustine, Irigaray shows that disincarnate images of eternity make for disincarnate ideals of language. Second, Irigaray's writing in *Marine Lover* attends to the family dynamics, divine and human, that shape communication. Language is always embedded in networks of relationship. Irigaray's dramatic presentation of this insight shines light on the pivotal role played by family dynamics in *De magistro*.

Irigaray reminds us that the stories we tell about origins matter—especially when it comes to the stories that shape our lives with language. Drawing on her psychoanalytic training, she invites us, her readers, to examine the stories we tell about our past, not to determine their truth or falsity, but to notice what they reveal about us. She invites us as well to remember the past—to reconfigure it, flesh it out, and give it a body. Her meditation on nativities and language in *Marine Lover* dovetails with Augustine's insight that my imagination for the nativity of my native tongue cannot but shape how I speak and what I say.[1] If I imagine my native language to have been birthed out of a need to get what I want from indifferent others, I will think of language primarily as a tool for making desires known. If I imagine my language to have been birthed out of a perfect internal articulacy into a shabby material world, I will feel frustrated in my attempts to get words to say what I mean. If I imagine my language has degenerated from something better and purer than ordinary human words, I will discipline and refine my speech to suit that abstract logic and its sublime offerings.

The opening lines of *Marine Lover* describe the sealing of Irigaray's lips and the impossibility of speaking with her imagined interlocutor. "How I should love you if to speak to you were possible."[2] *Marine Lover* is a love letter to the philosopher Friedrich Nietzsche. But even as it is a love letter, it is also a goodbye or a leave-taking from the man Irigaray indicts as being unable to love anyone but himself. In his writing, Nietzsche is explicitly concerned to find a feminine companion, whom he associates with the idea of *life*. Despite this avowed interest, Irigaray accuses Nietzsche of being unable to encounter real difference. She maintains that any feminine other Nietzsche loves is only himself. Every Nietzschean encounter with a feminine other collapses into sameness. Irigaray thus begins her engagement with him with a sense of the impossibility of discourse, the impossibility of speaking in her own feminine voice. She laments that she has been to Nietzsche only his "resonance," the drum amplifying his words.[3] She accuses Nietzsche of desiring to speak with a feminine other only so that he might hear his own voice echoing back into his ears. If he can make even her own words into an echo, what can she hope for when she speaks with him?

Irigaray's *Marine Lover* does not open with Augustine's question "What do we want to accomplish when we speak with one another?" Yet *Marine Lover*—and all Irigaray's writing—is haunted by it. This question motivates Irigaray's use of varied strategies for engaging her material and her reader. Like Augustine, Irigaray does not always straightforwardly say what she means. She does not speak to inform, and she finds playful ways to disrupt the informing speech of others. She tries to interrupt univocal and totalizing ways of speaking by "snipping the wires" of discourse[4] and "jamming the theoretical machinery [of discourse] itself, of suspending its pretension to the production of a truth and of a meaning that are excessively univocal."[5] Such a posture makes Irigaray maddeningly difficult to read—and richly rewarding. Instead of attempting to insert her own acts of understanding into readers' minds, she speaks to engage, to provoke, and to love. She invites her readers to respond with attention and creativity.[6]

In *Marine Lover*, Irigaray engages Nietzsche's critiques of history and Christian ressentiment, and she critiques the way he situates women in his writing. Yet instead of taking Nietzsche's most obviously disparaging comments about women head-on, she engages him using a strategy of "double mimesis" or talking back. As a writer, she takes up the position of the feminine as described by Nietzsche, inhabiting that posture within her speech. Her repetition undercuts the position the philosopher imposes on her, and as she speaks with him, she critiques the way Nietzsche has failed to encounter the feminine other he claims to desire. She deploys this strategy of double mimesis throughout her writing, Kelly Oliver explains, taking up "the position of the feminine allotted to women in the texts of Plato, Nietzsche, Freud, Lacan, Merleau-Ponty, Levinas, Heidegger, and others, by repeating their words back to them in the context of her own parodic and lyrical discourse. By so doing, she challenged the limited position assigned to woman as mere reflection of man, and opened up a space for another voice."[7]

Linking the feminine and the fluid, Irigaray writes *Marine Lover* from the point of view of water, from what Nietzsche seems to have appropriated and disregarded. In taking up that feminine subjectivity, she shows that Nietzsche failed to comprehend its originary, natal depths. "If, as Nietzsche's Zarathustra proclaims, the *Übermensch* is the 'meaning of the earth,' Irigaray's *Marine Lover* suggests that like the Christianity he criticizes, Nietzsche, too, has turned the earth (and the sea) into a tomb and mined its depths only to soar above it and leave it behind."[8] Her writing dives into those depths, finding them teeming with life. Irigaray speaks with Nietzsche in order to criticize the philosopher's failure to encounter sexual difference. Yet her speaking with him also presents invigorating new conceptions of life.

In *The Birth of Tragedy*, Nietzsche famously describes a fundamental struggle between the Apollonian and Dionysian drives. He argues that the tension between the two produced the great Greek tragedies. This artistic expression displayed, on Nietzsche's view, a joyous, life-affirming response to the suffering of the world. He contrasts this artistic expression with Christianity, which he accuses of being opposed to life, a form of nihilism that hates this world and is always looking for the next.[9] Irigaray reminds readers of *Marine Lover* that the stories of the incarnations of Dionysus and Apollo suggest an irreconcilable and tragic conflict between what is human and what is divine, as well as between what is masculine and what is feminine. In these tragic stories, women are sacrificed, annihilated, and made subservient, and they lose their ability to speak in their own voices. Nietzsche's claim that these stories are "life-affirming" is therefore dubious. Irigaray agrees with Nietzsche's hunch that femininity is tied up with life. But she maintains that whatever life Nietzsche finds in his philosophical project is suspect, given that the project has effectively written women out of the story. While Nietzsche accuses Christianity of being opposed to life, Irigaray turns the accusation on the philosopher himself.

Marine Lover displays a euphonious doubling of voices. In the final third of the book, Irigaray's response to Nietzsche is reprised within the stories of the incarnations of Dionysus, Apollo, and Christ. Her question— "Can I, a woman, speak with Nietzsche in a way that reaches him?"—is doubled in her mythic question "Can mortals speak with the Father-God?" And these questions are trebled in Augustine and Adeodatus's conversation in *De magistro*, where they discuss both how they talk with each other and how they listen to the voice of God. Both texts summon the reader to consider: Can I mean anything other than what I have been given to mean? What do we who position ourselves as masters—philosophical, theological, parental—want to accomplish when we speak? Do we want simply to inform? To hear ourselves reflected back? To grow in understanding or love? How, we might wonder, could our speaking with others become the birth of meaning?

To Irigaray's ear, the tragic works of art Nietzsche celebrates are not the paeans to life he supposes. In her lyrical retelling of the myth, Dionysus quickly learns of his father Zeus's divine indifference to earthly life. He learns as well to demand that mortals mortgage all human sense to an earthly beyond. He might be said to represent an extreme form of talking to inform, expressing the excesses of his father's power and indifference. Yet, tormented by the destruction and loss of his mother, he is consumed by desire for the earth and for bodies (especially women's bodies). His desire for what is earthly and mortal is in tragic conflict with his identity as the son of his divine father. The coming of the word from on high means the obliteration of all earthly meaning.

Irigaray reminds readers that Dionysus, though conceived in a mortal womb, does not gestate within his mother. While pregnant, she is immolated by a vision of her lover, and the fetal Dionysus is sewn within his immortal father's thigh to complete his period of gestation. Thus Dionysus is said to be "twice born." He is between two births, neither fully accomplished, such that he remains forever a child.[10] Dionysus's mortal body never grows up—he continues to nurse like a child—and he can never be at home on the earth. Now he requires an "eternal entourage" of women to protect him.[11] A mythic logic connects Dionysus's interrupted gestation with his proclivity to drunken *exstasis*, torn away from his roots in exultation. He stands outside himself, outside of or beyond his body. Ever the prodigal in exile from the site of his birth, he loses himself again and again in dissipation. He is unable to settle in either body or soul, and he moves ceaselessly between them.[12]

Dionysus longs for women and incites their desire because of his prematurely ended gestation within his mother. His second birth—his passage into the world—comes through Zeus's divine paternal power: "Miracle of divine power taking the place of the mother's birthing."[13] Zeus, most powerful of fathers, arrogates the power of procreation to himself because he cannot abide a procreative earth and the fostering of growth apart from himself. He wants his lightning—a terrifying, immolating flash—to "sire all genesis."[14] The coming of the god Dionysus is the annihilation of the mortal, of the earthly. The shock of his coming freezes life, keeping it, like Dionysus, from ever growing or changing, from becoming.[15] In place of the growth and change of mortal life, Zeus sets up a realm of fixity and stasis, and a longing for what is eternal.

This longing of Dionysus is never satisfied. He is always at a distance, still seeking even in exile. And he elicits this same desire within his followers. "He goes into bodies in order to empty them of substance, drink their blood, change them into divine longing."[16] When he comes, he leaves distance between mortals, and between mortals and the earth. Each reaches toward the heavens rather than toward the other.[17] The absence Dionysus sets up becomes a desire leading to death, and the women who follow Dionysus in their madness kill their own children.[18] The sacrifice signals the father's awful devaluation of life on earth. The sorrowing women are told their earthly pain is necessary and will be overcome. They are implicitly promised that, in the life to come, earthly pain will no longer matter. From the view of the gods, such pain is trifling and beneath notice.

Dionysus longs for his mortal mother, the site of his first "birth," but, Irigaray writes, "the love he brings to life is already the love of eternity."[19] When the father-god Zeus sends his word from on high, he does not want his word to take on flesh and become entangled with mortal life. The birth of Dionysus therefore incites a longing for eternity and an obliteration of the earth. Irigaray describes a cloud coming down from heaven, covering "every earthly shoot" so that the whole earth is "housed in a tomb of godly aspect."[20] With the arrival of Dionysus, divine sense blots out every human sense. Irigaray describes this occultation of human meaning:

> The god comes. And darkness covers the earth. Thick shadow blots out the sky. The ocean is unleashed. The earth shakes. And nothing is as it was. . . . The thunderbolt crashes. The god is there. Wrenching advent . . . And this is the beginning of the exodus toward the beyond. Life after death initiates the world. The word comes down from on high to start trying to distinguish good from bad, what the gods love from what they condemn.[21]

With the coming of Dionysus—"wrenching Advent"—the flood of Genesis gives way to the exodus of the chosen people. Why is the earth obliterated? Why do the people find themselves aliens in a land where they once were at home? Because the word came down from on high to distinguish good from bad, what is beloved of the gods from what is not. That word sends men and women into exile. Their own world becomes dark and senseless, and they look toward the heavens for meaning. They have failed in their attention and in their affection for the earth. They have given themselves to longing for eternity and for eternal meaning. Mortals may be a mixture of life and death, becoming and eternity, but after the arrival of the god Dionysus, the longing for eternity comes to predominate. "And today they can no longer see what was apparent to them yesterday. Opening up their eyes, they feel separated from the immediate that surrounds them. Opacity and insignificance cover and dwell in all things."[22] Torn away from their birth, they look for what is immortal and eternal, a heavenly world apart from earthly blossoming. "And love is that which, by separating them from themselves, draws them to suffer such agonies that the end of their divine destiny is accomplished. And from him whom they adore, they receive passage into the beyond."[23] The word from on high obliterates what is earthly, leaves mortals conflicted in their attachments to earthly loves, and demands fidelity to a promised future of static but potent perfection. "And all things live stretching upward, summoned out of their immediate surroundings. And each man is separated from the whole because he thus reaches up to the sky. And between each and every man stands the void created by the presence-absence of the god."[24] Because the incarnation of Dionysus is aborted, he is tormented by dissociation and alienation from what is fleshly and earthly, and his followers learn his torment.

The word of Zeus, as it arrives through Dionysus, is an extreme picture of talking to inform, a way of speaking in which the speaker, Zeus, is more preoccupied with sublime achievements of articulation than with speaking with—reaching and touching—another. The word of Zeus comes like a bolt of lightning. It arrives from on high but also out of nowhere, and it is indifferent to where it lands or what it destroys. It does not aim to speak with or create a connection with another, but only dazzles or destroys. It does not emerge out of faithfulness to mortals or to the earth. Instead its source is a boundless power of perfect articulacy. Nothing about this expression of power nourishes or connects with those mortals who, having received the divine call, sacrifice themselves to what is eternal and otherworldly.

Zeus's word, Dionysus, is sent to earth only as a call to the world beyond.[25] In this way, the story of Dionysus echoes a problematic picture of the inner teacher that we examined in chapter 1—the inner teacher as disincarnate Truth who calls souls to turn away from each other and toward a heavenly beyond. Zeus sends Dionysus to turn the desire of mortals heavenward, to teach them to withhold their attention and affection from earthly creatures. Like Dionysus, we may be tempted to believe our maternal inheritance is only an opaque and dispiriting life in the body and time, while our father's eternal life promises an escape from competition, isolation, scarcity, and finitude. Persuaded that knowledge has nothing to do with suffering, patience, or times of darkness, we may feel ourselves summoned toward abstraction, far from time, touch, and sorrow. We may be tempted to imagine that our words are most perfect when they enable minds to hook up with what is eternal and immutable, and we may be drawn toward speaking in a way that stands apart from all patterns of growth, love, and mortal life. We may even abandon all earthly sense or meaning, because it seems to have no value, compared with eternity's crystalline clarity. If we fall prey to such a temptation, we have learned the lesson Zeus teaches through his son, Dionysus. It goes without saying that this view is certainly not Augustine's. It is not Christian either. Yet the prejudice toward disincarnating views of language is not unmotivated.

Dionysus's implicit promise is that the death of the earth, together with the deaths of mortals and of mortal attachments, will have eternal meaning that can never be lost. In Irigaray's story of Dionysus, the true life is the life to come. There—where all will be well—the meaning of mortal life, suffering, and death will be perfectly clear and intelligible. Nietzsche scorns just this sort of cosmic justification. Yet while he criticizes this vision of sacrifice and redemption as a corrupt Christian story, Augustine and Irigaray find alternative versions of the Christian story to tell. As we will see in future chapters, they propose forms of communication between gods and humans that do not demand this wholesale sacrifice of human life, love, and meaning.

Though Dionysus and Apollo are both Zeus's sons and messengers, they differ substantially. Yet Irigaray's lyrical retelling of the myth of Apollo echoes problematic accounts of Augustine's inner teacher too. Though Dionysus is the word of Zeus, Apollo is that word more perfectly. More self-controlled and more articulate, Apollo is the messenger who ensures that the divine father's word is delivered. Apollo arrives to proclaim the will of his father, Zeus, and the time of Apollo is the time when the god speaks. "And the son, as soon as he comes into the world, is spokesman for his Father."[26] No longer are mortals left to decipher dreams or earthly signs. The god will henceforth make himself known only through words. Men will learn to relate to each other through words as well. Transmitting the god's will with only a word is Apollo's great art.

Unlike Dionysus, who remains a child, Apollo arrives in the world already mature. He walks and talks from the time he is born, and he lives an ordered and measured life. Apollo does not walk on the wild side like Dionysus nor communicate by thunderbolt like Zeus. Though he is the god of war, Apollo often acts gently. He sends forth inspired words that slip into minds unnoticed, leaving the affected mortals with only the vaguest sense of celestial intervention. Irigaray describes Apollo's arrival:

> The divine enters the world surreptitiously. No break-ins, no bloodshed. At least in general, at least not visibly or even tangibly. In this way *Apollo establishes the Olympian regime which will rule over men by means of a voice that speaks to them from within.* The empire of the Father of the gods is founded by a mutation in the nature of signs. The mediator par excellence between heaven and earth, earth and heaven, will henceforth be the word. The God's sovereignty is installed through the privilege given to the word over any other system of exchange.[27]

Apollo comes as the word, but not the word made flesh. If he has a body, it is, Irigaray writes, a "mineral body,"[28] not a body given by a mortal mother. Born of divine parents, Apollo has a bodily appearance, yet he is not fully incarnate. His divine presence is never expressed as a life in time. His beauty draws one toward a divine presence "mediated and generalized" that may ultimately be subsumed into a more and more abstract idea. Irigaray writes, "Theophany of the god of speech. Still cosmic, still of the senses. In which the triumph of the speculative is already heralded."[29] Apollo's speech draws one toward what is divine, but this divinity will not be encountered through touch nor earthly signs. Rather the divine becomes something speculative, perfected, and fixed. Even though the god comes so close with his words, right into an interior realm, the mortal to whom he speaks is never touched, and there is no intimacy between the two. The soul is "a mere place of passive receptivity between 'God' and men."[30] The kingdom of the word allows the god to get inside mortal minds. But through the insertion of his message, writes Irigaray, Apollo bewitches mortal minds with an abstracted idea. His idea lives within them, but it remains fundamentally foreign and invasive.

Apollo is a god of separation, differentiation, and articulation. Having shirked his own body, flesh is always alien to him, and he must borrow the flesh of others to distinguish himself. He articulates and differentiates himself through speech and through his naming of himself. He seeks perfection through a facile and flawless power of articulation, but that power allows him only to love and seek what is the same. "This god does not reach out to the other, is not prolifically fertile, but uses his strength to mold shapes until they are perfect."[31] He cannot even reach out a kindred hand of acknowledgment to his twin sister, Artemis, who helped birth him into life, and whose role is forever to "serve as midwife to sons and brothers of light, who own the gift of speech."[32] She is a mere reflection of him. She is the moon, which reflects the light of the sun but has no claim to its own brilliance.

Apollo's task is the reproduction of the will of the father, and his unvoiced words are his instruments for placing his father's idea within the minds and hearts of mortals. He is the god of the lyre and the bow, two instruments that work only when held in perfect tension, stroked with meticulous attention. Apollo's possession of these two instruments suggests he knows the art of enchantment as well as the art of polemic, and Irigaray wonders whether he uses the former to cover over the latter.[33] He rules through a quiet voice from within, not through external pressure, demands, or argumentation. He transmits his word instantaneously, softly slipping that word into mortal minds. The mortal to whom the god speaks cannot distinguish between his own speech and the speech of the god, so subtle and smooth is the implantation. Apollo breathes his heavenly messages into mortal ears with such a surreptitious art that they are immediately assimilated by recipients, who offer neither resistance nor response. Yet his charm hides acts of warfare, because these gently implanted words bring destruction. Zeus sends Apollo as messenger in order to set up his Olympian kingdom. Apollonian teaching is a disguised act of war, and the redemption it offers will never be known by the many slain in the march toward the kingdom.

Irigaray's picture of Apollo recalls those commentators who would make Augustine's inner teacher into a mind-fixer who bypasses the fragile exigencies of human words in order to fix two minds on one thought. Like that inner teacher, Apollo exercises a subtle power of mind control. He informs without dialogue, insinuating his father's message into mortal beings whose life he neither knows nor cares for. Neither Apollo nor his words are ever truly incarnate. The word he brings from Zeus takes its meaning only from what is divine and immutable, not from the earth nor from human life. His status of being just beyond the body allows him to communicate the divine message unsullied by earthly entanglements that might muddy his message. His word—fully mature and irrefutably clear—arrives to replace human words, with their ambiguity, equivocity, and layers of meaning. Apollo's word purports to have the perfection of eternity, but it is drained of life and meaning. Apollo's story reminds us that a divine word, sent from an impassable divine father to usurp and make nonsense of human words, is too immaterial and otherworldly to find any place in our ears, on our tongues, and in our hearts. Likewise, if we imagine Augustine's inner teacher to arrive like Apollo, quietly informing minds with an eternal divine word, we will have no hope of understanding the significance of the words we speak with each other, for they will have none.

Irigaray tells the story of the birth of one more god—Christ—and she tells it under two guises. We take up the second in a future chapter. Here we look at her first, Nietzschean account of Christ. This Christ is one more god who speaks to inform. Irigaray begins by decrying what she terms the common interpretation of the Annunciation and the birth of Christ: "This mysterious conception leads, first of all, to the repudiation of the woman in which it takes place."[34] This Christ-child is the father's word, who comes from on high and returns there. He looks only to the father. He feels no gravitational pull toward earth, nor toward his mother from whom he was born.

On this model, man finds his salvation by following the apparent paradigm of Christ: looking to the will and the speech of his father. Christ maintains this allegiance because his deepest fear is to be forsaken by the father.[35] And so his attraction to mother, wife, and other women fades. But while Christ does not seek them, women seek him; they are attentive and receptive, softly and submissively listening with joy. "Are they nothing but ears?" wonders Irigaray.[36] The women have just enough of a body to follow him, but their desires for human goods are cast off in their hope of receiving a heavenly blessing.

In this suppression of desire and speech, women imitate the (Nietzschean) Mary that Irigaray critiques. Mary is a receptacle who welcomes and "reproduces only the will of the Father."[37] She listens but does not speak. She is a chalice—a faithful receptacle—that receives the overflow of the love of the father, but she has no maternal character, no creative role

within the life of her son. She receives her child, but he is not acknowledged as her own. She is merely an instrument facilitating Christ's earthly
walk. She is a tight-lipped receptacle who was favored with a word, a word
to which God demanded that she sacrifice her flesh.

Mary's *yes* to the message of the father was simultaneously a *no* to her
own life, to her own flourishing, to her own desire. Denying everything except the word and the will of the father (the only thing she can reproduce),
she undergoes her own crucifixion and death, prefiguring Christ's. "Ob-
scurely, she is in mourning for belonging to the earth-mother and to her
sexual body. This is her cross in life, this double closure of her lips, upon
which is implanted the visible erection of his passion."[38] She is no longer a
source of generation and life, but simply a "vehicle for the Other." Though
she lives forever, she also knows death, just as her son would. Indeed, when
Christ dies, death is claimed to be Life. She takes comfort in the knowledge
that her death has meant life for the world. But once Christ has arrived,
lived, and returned to heaven, Mary, his very condition for life on earth,
is forgotten or hidden.

In this story, Christ's passage to life runs not through his mortal
mother but through his suffering, death, and return to his immortal paternal origin. Mary, obscured, becomes the dumb instrument of conception, and her title as *Mother of God* is thin. She is the means by which man
and God are reconciled, but the *how* of her mediation is underdetermined.
Christ is the way, the truth, and the life, and the redemptive path he lays
out runs through his paternal inheritance: "Become the Father's Word,
and accept agony and crucifixion as passages from incarnation into eternal life."[39] Like Dionysus and Apollo, this Christ draws his followers into a
heavenly beyond. But Christ does not offer a redemption by way of rapture
(Dionysus) or of quiet enchantment (Apollo), and he makes no promise
of a life without horror. On this reading of his incarnation, Christ demonstrates that the way to overcome the pain of living is through pain. Passion
and death usher in the Kingdom, and Christ's followers may be ushered
into eternal bliss through them. This passion is the glory of the father.

This story gives us one more picture of talking to inform. In this
reading, Mary's suffering of a word—her reception of the teaching of the
father-god—is her greatest glory. The father is the teacher, and Mary is the
receptacle for his teaching. As a god, the father's power of self-expression

is unconstrained and unmatched. The father-god is a teacher—a master really—who expresses his will irresistibly. This god puts his (already-formed) Word within Mary, and she serves as holding place until she can give the very same back to the father. God's Word is not informed nor changed by its time within the matrix that supposedly engendered it. Mary receives the expression of the will of the father and dies to herself in her fidelity to reproducing that will. But she is no co-creator of that Word; she has no communion with the father over their child. The meaning of the Word belongs fully to the father. Her voice and her response are not her own. She only echoes back to the father his own voice. Mary carries the burden of the divine message, and she is complicit in God's use of language as a tool for making himself understood. This is no picture of communication, but rather of informing and being informed.

When we read the coming of Christ like this, he—the Word—is something like the father's best idea, impassive to what is earthly, mortal, and fleshly. Even the apparent suffering of the Word on the cross is an illusion, obscured by the cloud of glory that carries him off to heaven. In this retelling of Christ's story, Christ, the so-called incarnate Word, is just as alienated from life in time as were Dionysus and Apollo. He quickly returns to the realm of his sovereignty, unaffected by a life in time.

Irigaray's double mimesis of Nietzsche's story about Christianity raises questions about this constellation of power, gender, incarnation, and meaning. Does the fact of being incarnate make life with language more or less alienating? Does incarnation impede our efforts to inform others with perfect clarity? Are the trappings of mortal life a damnable drag on thinking things? Irigaray asks, "*Et incarnatus est*. Must this coming be univocally understood as a redemptory submission of the flesh to the Word? Or else: as the Word's faithfulness to the flesh?"[40] Does the Word seek the flesh? Or does it drown out human life and meaning, announcing the futility of other words?

Irigaray wonders whether mortals can mean only what they are given to mean by God. Reading *Marine Lover* in conjunction with *De magistro* highlights the problem of divine overdetermination of the meaning of signs, where the word mediates between God and mortals, but God controls the meaning of that word absolutely. This represents a problem not only for mortals but for God, too. Overdetermination of the meaning of signs is problematic, not because mortals may be flattened under the thumb of a tyrannical father like Zeus. Tyranny is not the most descriptive language for what is at stake. In a Christian context, the troubles of divine life center less on tyrannical attempts to secure obedience from creatures and more on the difficulty of eliciting their attention and affection. God suffers from a thwarted longing for intimacy. Perhaps what God longs for most of all is conversation, a real exchange, words and individuals to which God could be responsive. If God fully determines the meaning of human signs, then we can never really mean anything. But I suspect God would be no less tormented by that situation than we would be.

Irigaray shows us how all three gods—Dionysus, Apollo, and Christ—can be read as disincarnating ideals of speech and communication. They can be read as bad ideals of the relationship between what is divine and what is mortal, where mortal beings serve only to receive and reproduce what is given them. These stories run parallel to the contemporary readings of the inner teacher we encountered in chapter 1. As readers of *De magistro*, we are not beholden to the stories of Dionysus and Apollo, to be sure. Yet our stake in the story of Christ is different. Augustine casts Christ, son of the father, as the inner teacher, whose teaching forms an end to the dialogue Augustine and his son enjoy. The Christ that Irigaray critiques evokes the inhuman ways of informing that Augustine implicitly criticizes in *De magistro*. We must ask, therefore, whether there is another way of conceiving of Christ and the activity of the inner teacher. Irigaray's writing helps steer us away from problematic ways of describing Augustine's inner teacher, even as she asks her readers her own versions of Augustine's questions: What kind of desire underlies our speaking with one another? Do we want, most of all, to escape the life we share, in favor of some privileged beyond? Or do we seek connection with others and with God? Can we find, in that connection, acknowledgments of faithfulness and love?

PART 2

INTIMATES

CHAPTER FOUR

DELIVERANCE

Irigaray dramatizes the world-weary temptation to replace time with eternity and to replace body with spirit—and to think the replacement is an upgrade in our ability to know. This temptation is not far from what poet Ellen Hinsey calls "*Temptation Disguised as Thought* / To follow an argument, abstractly, to its conclusion."[1] Thinking does involve abstraction and tracing arguments to conclusions. The *temptation* is to believe (mistakenly) that we can know the truth best when we have left behind what is concrete. Even though *De magistro* dramatizes this temptation, it is easy to read the dialogue from within the grip of it. We might approach the dialogue looking to find the "real argument" apart from the apparently superficial details of the text. We identify the main points of the argument: "We talk to inform." "We talk to be informed." "All words are signs. They point minds to contemplation of things." But if we gather the scattered lines of argument, trying to fit them into a direct trajectory, we miss the mark. We will find ourselves looking beyond the concrete beings Adeodatus and Augustine, looking beyond the concrete richness of the literary allusions, and looking beyond the shared life father and son bring to the conversation. It is little wonder what this interpretative abstraction yields by way of conclusions: a bloodless power of God, Christ the Truth, the only successful meaning-fixer.

We will know the tug of the temptation dramatized in *De magistro* insofar as we are beholden to the prejudice that time and bodies are hopeless impediments to intelligibility. This prejudice is neither stupid nor unmotivated. We may have felt that words and thoughts are trapped inside own minds, inaccessible to those in other bodies. We try to offer up expressions of wonder or joy or grief or desire, only to find that our words miss the mark, fail to connect us with others. Or we chisel out perfect words only to find the moment has passed. It is difficult to make our way with words in a world where things come and go, decay, refuse to stay in place. Few understand these heartbreaking difficulties better than Augustine, the man with the absent lover and the dead son. Time and bodies open us to the possibilities of failed connections and sorrowful loss, seemingly blocking communication. We are tempted to think we know abstractly, by getting our minds in touch with *what is*. As we try to inform other minds, the hungry, sick, tired, lust-leashed, mortal body appears to be a drag on that mind-meld.

We began with Augustine's question: what are we trying to accomplish when we speak with one another? The dialogue also implicitly raises the question: what do we make of our failures to achieve the ends we have in mind? I have promised *De magistro* is no lament for ineffectual words—rounded off with a stopgap solution in the form of Christ. Instead *De magistro* is an invitation to look again at what we are about with words. It is true that words do not always allow us to accomplish what we want. They often fail us in our attempts to connect or console or instruct. Our communication falls well short of our visions of perfection. Augustine invites us to ask ourselves how we relate to that apparent failure: What do the limits of our words tell us about how we can live with them—and with each other?

I called the temptation world-weary, but readers of the dialogue will remember that neither father nor son seems particularly wearied. They joke and tease and reflect together at leisure. Though there are moments of puzzlement where the two struggle to make sense of each other, the exchange is intimate and familiar. The tone hints that there is more to the drama than the apparent philosophical moves. The familiarity of father and son makes some of the lines of argument ring false—and rightly so. Augustine dramatizes the temptation to think we talk only to teach or inform, but the conversation reveals that neither Augustine nor Adeodatus have truly fallen under the sway of that temptation. Augustine shows how rich with meaning is the life father and son share.

We return now to Augustine's metaphor of parturition that occurs midway through the dialogue. Augustine suggests Adeodatus may be wondering whether their discussion is bringing forth (*parturire*) something great or worthy. The metaphor rewards careful attention: *parturire* means to be in labor or to be pregnant with, as in the English word *parturition*. Augustine tells Adeodatus that they, father and son, are involved in a kind of birth. Their conversation about signs and signification is a reflection on what it is to live in that region (*regio*) where the blessed life is. Their conversation prepares them with exercises so that they will be able not only to fill their lungs with the air of the beata vita but to make their home there. Augustine says he is trying to prepare them not only to withstand (*sustinere*) but truly to love (*amare*) the heat and light (*calorem ac lucem*) of that life.[2] Augustine's words evoke the moment of a newborn's first gasps. This is the language of birth, of deliverance. Augustine hopes he and his son will not merely get a squinting glimpse of that dazzling realm, but will learn to love what gives light to the blessed life. It is a poignant image, but a strange one too. Tangled in knotty details of the conversation about signification and informing, we, Augustine's readers, may wonder what living the blessed life has to do with anything.[3]

We might think Augustine is interested in the happy life because this present life with language is perpetually dissatisfying. In that case, we would expect Augustine's sense of the blessed life to be given shape by his sense of the limits of his bodily life. We might expect the promise of the happy life to be mind-melding intelligibility, a place where we can escape the opacity the body seems to interpose between one mind and another. We might think Augustine's sense of spirit arises out of a sense of dissatisfaction with the body, or out of a painful awareness of the gaps and hesitations of mortal life. If Augustine shows the impossibility of a certain ideal of intelligibility, perhaps he is stuck reaching for an inner escape (with the time-preempting disincarnate word) or to an otherworldly escape (with the promise all will be made clear eschatologically). Because I do not read the dialogue as *lament* for the ineffectuality of words, it is not surprising I believe Augustine has a different sort of happy life at heart to share.

The metaphor of birth is the heart of the dialogue's logic. Something or someone is being born. But what? On the one hand, the conversation gives birth to deeper insight about why they talk with one another. Father and son's developing view of language—that is, we speak primarily to inform—will soon show its deficiencies, when they come to agree that Christ is the teacher of all. On the other hand, and much more fundamentally, the conversation gives birth to *them*, father and son. Recently baptized, they know their pilgrim lives are not their true end, and they look forward to the life of the blessed in heaven. They are not yet fully born into the life of Christ that they share. They are still being formed, not yet ready to withstand the heat and light of that most blessed realm. Yet they are moving toward the blessed life, from darkness to light, as they speak together about speaking.

Augustine's metaphor of parturition implies that the conversation in *De magistro* is not merely instrumental and informative, but generative. Augustine's speaking does not serve a narrowly instrumental purpose of informing Adeodatus about the nature of the beata vita. No human being could give a comprehensive account of that life. More importantly, no one reaches the beata vita through simply being informed about it. Augustine's own biography makes this painfully clear. Like every other form of human life, the beata vita is reached only through birth, which is hardly a process one can engineer or manage for oneself. What do we want in speaking together? Augustine's metaphor hints at an answer: We want to birth each other into the beata vita. The suggestion that the beata vita is reached through birth is not a surprising claim—at least not surprising to Christians. But his claim that conversation is part of that birth invites further investigation. It suggests an essential connection between word and life. It challenges the notion that intelligibility can exist apart from intimacy and connection with bodies, loves, times, and histories. The fact that conversation prepares us for the beata vita suggests that it is not a static reality, but one we are invited to form, in conversation with God and with others.

No intelligibility comes apart from intimacy. Augustine suggests as much, not only in *De magistro*, but in two related descriptions of blessedness in *Confessiones* 7 and 8.[4] Both episodes can be framed as a kind of birth or deliverance, where Augustine comes to a more expansive understanding of the intimacy he seeks. In *Confessiones* 7, Augustine wrestles with the temptation to know God apart from time and bodies, to set intelligibility and intimacy at odds. His encounter with God is unstable, however, and he falls back to earth. In *Confessiones* 8, Augustine tries again to move toward God, aided by his memories of intimacy, and he receives the light of security. Throughout the *Confessiones*, Augustine confesses his desire to love and be loved, and he details how his heart's capacity for love is dilated through his encounters with others. That dilation allows for his birth into a life most blessed.

We begin with a story of intelligibility and its apparent antagonist. In *Confessiones* 7, Augustine works to understand both the origin of evil and his own origin. His perplexity leads him to seek clarity in a vision that separates—absolutely—spirit from flesh. *Confessiones* 7 dramatizes a soul's ascent through a series of steps or exercises to what looks to be the ultimate vision: a view of Truth, clear and shining. It is a beautiful sight, but Augustine finds he cannot stay very long with this vision, and he crashes back to earth under the weight of what he terms his sexual habit (*consuetudo carnalis; conf.* 7.17.23). Rather than looking to assign blame for his fall from illumination—indicting a dragging body or an inconstant heart—we might consider what this apparent failure signals. Part of the work in this chapter will be to understand what kind of role Augustine's body and his sexual desire played in bringing him back down to earth. Augustine's sexual habit can be cast as a villain, a weak link in his capacity for knowing and loving God. But this typecasting may hide the complexity motivating the loss of the vision. The life most blessed, the divine life to which we aspire, may turn out to be quite otherwise than we anticipate. The blessed life may have something to do with the darkness the soul tries to put out of mind. In Augustine's case, that darkness contains a memory of intimate belonging. The memory pulls him away from his vision of perfect clarity, but arguably also delivers him into a more blessed life. Perfect intelligibility is not quite the revelation Augustine hoped for. The vision is not one Augustine could live with. He has yet to be delivered into a life with others.

Confessiones 7 opens with Augustine's struggle over how to conceive of God. He knows enough not to think of God as possessing the shape of the human body. He had always shunned that idea, even as a Manichee, and he is glad to find mother church agrees with him on that point (*conf.* 7.1.1). Though he knows not why, it is clear and certain to him that what is perishable is inferior to what is imperishable, that what is violable is inferior to what is inviolable, and that what can be changed is inferior to what is unchanging. Despite his conviction that God is "imperishable, inviolable, and immutable," Augustine must beat back the images of God that swarm his mind (*conf.* 7.1.1). Though he does not see God in the shape of a human body, he imagines God to be something physical, diffused through space, perhaps permeating all of creation as water surrounds and fills a sponge (*conf.* 7.5.7). Though he knows that God is not a material being, his imagination nonetheless generates images of God.

This misconception about God leaves Augustine with his old problem: finding an adequate explanation for the existence of evil. He had abandoned the Manichaean explanation, which posited a great race of darkness working in opposition to God, but he struggles to find an alternative explanation. If God created good creatures, and if God surrounds and fills all creation such that no bit of the created order lacks the presence of God, it seems difficult to explain how evil came into being and where it continues to exist (*conf.* 7.5.7). Surely God did not create it. Nor does it make sense to say God might have created using material with some element of evil in it. Yet if God is good and the source of everything in the created order, it seems hard to escape the conclusion God is the source of evil. If evil is a substance, either God is not the creator of all, or God is not fully good and powerful (*conf.* 7.5.7).

For Augustine, these are not merely academic questions. He worries that evil, especially the evil he himself has done, is incompatible with the fact of God's goodness. Augustine's earlier attempt to explain the source of evil by making himself the source of sin through his errant will only pushes the problem back: if God, the supreme good, made Augustine, whence comes Augustine's power to will evil and reject the good (*conf.* 7.3.5)? Why would his will pull him from the source of his life? Does God have any real power over evil? These questions revolve in Augustine's breast, and he labors to give birth to some account of his separation from his creator, some explanation for the sins that press down and oppress him: "What labor pains—what moans!—racked my heart, O my God."[5] Augustine has no clear vision of God and no clear vision of himself.

His torment is eased when he is caught up in a vision of a beautiful immaterial God. Under the tutelage of some Platonist books, Augustine turns inward where he sees a great light of truth that gives momentary relief to his perplexity. The books of the Platonists allow Augustine to conceive of God as immaterial. The vision of an immaterial God gives rest to Augustine's perplexity about the origins of evil. It resolves his misapprehensions that evil is some kind of substance and that God is diffused in space. Augustine no longer must think that the fact of evil undermines God's goodness. The God he loves is not a fantasy. Augustine is not mistaken when he says that he loves God and not just a figment of his imagination (*conf.* 7.17.23). Yet while his perplexity is somewhat relieved, the revelation does not show Augustine how to make his home in the patria nor how to be a divine son. In fact, Augustine says that he, who was supposedly doing the seeing, does not yet exist. His relief is accompanied by an air of unreality.

The light of truth Augustine sees is not an everyday kind of light, nor a brighter version of ordinary light. It is utterly different, Augustine explains, from the visible light we encounter: "Anyone who knows truth knows it, and anyone who knows it, knows eternity. Charity knows it."[6] This is what Augustine finds when he enters the innermost places of his being: a beautiful, disincarnate light known by anyone who knows truth. He who knows truth knows this light, and he who knows this light knows eternity. Augustine gets a vision of God, whom he describes as "eternal Truth, true Charity, and precious Eternity" (*conf.* 7.10.16).

Though this utterly different immaterial light is alleged to be Augustine's source, he finds himself very far from it. He sees the immaterial God only from afar, in what he calls a region of dissimilarity (*regio dissimilitudinis*; *conf.* 7.10.16). Standing in that nonplace, he takes himself to be unlike God and unlike creation (*conf.* 7.10.16). Given that those two options exhaust the possibilities of existing things, it is no surprise Augustine would say he who was doing the seeing does not yet exist. The region in which Augustine finds himself is utterly unlike ordinary, created experience. Augustine is shown perfect existence—but he is also shown that he does not yet exist. Augustine therefore describes himself as not yet capable of seeing this vision in its fullness. He can only squint at the disincarnate light.

Within this place of dissimilarity, Augustine hears God's voice from on high (*conf.* 7.10.16; Wetzel trans.): "I am the food of grown-ups; grow and you will feed on me. You will not change me into you, as you do the food of your flesh, but you will be changed into me."[7] James Wetzel proposes two ways to read this image: "The kind of feeding that changes the feeder into the source of food is either a form of starvation, where the body is forced to feed upon itself, or it is a gestation, a feeding from within the womb."[8] Wetzel opts for the image of a soul's gestation: as Augustine tries to define his difference from his heavenly father and take responsibility for that difference (in his unaccountable turn from God),[9] he is given a vision of himself as still in gestation, "awaiting a life-defining deliverance from [his] source."[10] If Augustine is indeed gestating in God, then he really does have his origin in God—a truth that the fact of his sin had caused him to doubt. The vision serves to release Augustine from a burden of responsibility for differentiation, through his sin.[11]

The promise of perfect intelligibility in *Confessiones* 7 is accompanied by the image of a soul yet unborn. The soul, insofar as it is anywhere at all, is in a metaphorical, immaterial womb—a kind of citadel. At first blush, the womb—weirdly unattached to any mothering body—might look like a nice place to live. It is furnished with the comforts of safety and clarity and walled up in clearly delineated boundaries. Since this womb looks to Augustine (momentarily) like the one place where God is seen and known, we might guess he would be in no hurry to leave. To an inhabitant of this perfected place, leaving it looks like a descent into separation and death, into frustration and failure—and away from the presence of God. Yet, if we read the *regio dissimilitudinis* as a womb, the internal logic of the image tells that Augustine will ultimately be delivered. A womb is no place to stay.

It is possible to read *Confessiones* 7 as reinforcing persistent prejudices about the relative value of bodily life in the pursuit of knowledge and the love of God. The vision seems to trade on an absolute difference between spirit and flesh. Augustine's clearest vision of God and Truth comes apart from creation and, most poignantly, apart from those created beings Augustine felt to be bone of his bone. This vision suggests the happy life is a life free from darkness and hesitation, where one knows with perfect clarity and without ambiguity. In such a place, intimacy is simply the suspension of material difference such that two minds can be transparent to one another. They can escape the stuttering of ordinary human speech and the chaos of human life through a perfect hookup.

If knowledge comes only on these terms, human beings will have a tough time of it. A standard reading of *Confessiones* 7 might say Augustine has a glimmer of perfect intelligibility when he gets a vision of a disincarnate God, but his body and his sexual desire drag him back down to mundane reality and away from his beautiful vision.[12] Augustine's connection with an immaterial God is apparently severed when his body reasserts itself in its desire for more flesh and for other flesh—for what gives no illumination. On this (mistaken) reading, the body has once again intruded between Augustine and knowledge, between Augustine and intelligibility, and between Augustine and deliverance. If sexual desire is what drags Augustine away from knowing God, he will need a greater power of will to keep flesh from being a drag on spirit. He will need to put on the willpower of Jesus Christ and to quit paying attention to his desire to be intimate with others. If Augustine wants to be able to remain with the God of the books of the Platonists, he will need to be infused with the power of a Christ who never had to grow up, who never lived with a finite, darkened human mind. That son of God certainly never suffered the indignity of having a body drag him back from knowing his immaterial Father.

Kathleen Skerrett sensitively charts Augustine's ambivalence about his vision of an immaterial God.[13] On the one hand, Augustine finds the vision a relief. He sees that he has his origin in God, in that light that is the very source of his life. Furthermore, he finds the fact that he and God are both immaterial allows for a closeness that would be impossible if both were only material beings. God's creation of Augustine out of nothing leaves God and Augustine radically *materially* differentiated, untouchable one to the other. Skerrett writes, "The doctrine of a material God made nonsense of the possibility that God could get 'inside' Augustine, to that depth of unlikeness where Augustine would discover in himself an astonishing love already loving."[14] Before the vision of *Confessiones* 7, it seemed to Augustine that two material beings (one perfect, one made ex nihilo) could never meaningfully reach each other. Therefore, when Augustine is taken up into a vision of an immaterial God, his sense of separation from God is suspended. This suspension of separation seems to him like a real connection with the God for whom he had been longing. But the wide difference between a lack of material separation and a true intimacy soon presses itself.

Skerrett's interpretation insists on the importance of reading Augustine's confession as confession. Augustine has been worried not only about some generic problem of evil but about *his* entanglements with evil. In his vision, God is good. God is That Which Is—the real stuff—and God is immaterial. But if That Which Is is immaterial, all Augustine's material entanglements would be, at bottom, nothing. Augustine's vision of God apart from creation implies creation is nothing—nothing good, nothing of substance. Augustine's life and past fade into darkness compared to that shining light, beaming on Augustine's face and beating back his feeble gaze. Augustine confesses his temptation to turn inward to find God in a realm apart from material goods, a realm apart from the material traces one body leaves on another, a realm apart from loving mortal beings. It was perhaps tempting for Augustine to think that all his material entanglements (his sins, the partner he had loved and sent away, his failures of friendship and love) were nothing. The spirit-body split holds out the promise of knowledge apart from grief and darkness and sin, but this promise is a false, faithless ideal.

While this God seems to Augustine to be exactly what he has been sighing after, Augustine's clarity is accompanied by a peculiar vertigo.[15] Skerrett presses: why does Augustine still feel the intensity of his carnal desire in the midst of his beautiful vision of God? Augustine has seen Truth with perfect clarity. He has encountered the God who can give relief to his questioning. He has come to see his origin in this truth, and his former intimacies seemed to fade. If Augustine truly thinks he has seen God apart from creation, whatever he might be drawn back to cannot be anything good. Yet if those things Augustine has left behind in his ecstasy are nothing—if they mean nothing in the face of the perfectly intelligible and eternal Truth Augustine has encountered—why do they still have power over him?

To answer the question, we look to the possibilities conserved in the memory that drags Augustine back to earth. Something about his habitual ways of providing for his flesh made it impossible for Augustine to remain with his vision of God. Skerrett highlights the conjunction of the thought of an immaterial God and the pull of what is often translated as *sexual habit* (*consuetudo carnalis*; *conf.* 7.17.23). Skerrett warns against interpreting *consuetudo carnalis* simply in terms of physical compulsiveness. This counterweight in Augustine is tied up with his memory of his worldly attachments—a memory he cannot disavow. "If we strictly construe this confession [of *consuetudo carnalis*] as evidence of the severity of his temptation, then we will miss the clamor of grief and joy that his sexual habit conserved—the memory of an intimate belonging that seemed to drag most heavily when he aspired to embrace an immaterial God."[16] A vision of the beauty of an immaterial God seems irreconcilable with Augustine's good memory of the relationships that interrupted his sense of self-secured integrity and unconstrained will. That memory was a reminder of his erotic desire and of his "belonging through his own incompleteness to the incompleteness of others."[17] This memory reminds Augustine that whatever he secures with this immaterial truth will be nothing like that intimacy he once knew. Nor will the knowledge he encounters in the *Confessiones* 7 vision be like the knowledge in which his old intimacies held him. I do not mean to suggest the old intimacy was perfect—not by any means. But it calls Augustine back down to earth and prevents him from shrugging off his past in the midst of his hookup with Truth.

In the moment when Augustine is desperate to know God, he is reminded of another knowledge: that of the first man, who exclaims the woman is bone of his bone and flesh of his flesh. Augustine's temptation to misconstrue the gift of his flesh as nothing more than a gnawing hunger stands at odds with the memory of the intimacies he had known—memories of fullness, and not merely lack, memories of natal, sexual, familial, and other forms of intimacy. Those connections were ways of knowing too. Such memories draw him back from a dazzling vision of Truth where he knows alone, far from God. He cannot pretend those connections meant nothing, though as aspiring convert he must have been tempted to try. God's creatures may have been created ex nihilo, but, Skerrett suggests, it may be more fruitful to think of creation taking its origin from *depth*.[18] Augustine's descent to earth during his vision of God suggests the darkness is not nothing, but a form of plenitude. It is a revelation of God.

In his postmortem on the vision, Augustine reflects on the difference between presumption and confession, or between "those who see where they would go but do not see the way to it—the way to our blessed home [*beatificam patriam*], which is a place not just to perceive but live in."[19] In both *De magistro* and *Confessiones*, Augustine hopes not merely to get a fleeting glimpse of the beata vita. He wants to learn how to live there. And *there* will not be a region of dissimilarity. Whatever understanding of truth was given him in the vision of an immaterial God was not one Augustine could live in nor one he could live with. When he has the vision, Augustine does not yet fully have a life, let alone a happy one. He is gestating in God, and the image of gestation has its own organic movement. A womb is a good place to originate, but it is no place to live.

Augustine's understanding of divine life at this point is evident in the way he describes Christ. Augustine confesses in *Confessiones* 7 he thought Christ was a man of great wisdom who had authority in teaching because of his disdain for temporal goods for the sake of attaining immortality. He thought Christ was authoritative because he had managed to put off concern for temporal goods in pursuit of wisdom (*conf.* 7.19.25). That is, Christ had seemingly been able to do precisely what Augustine had been unable to do since his desire for wisdom had been kindled at the age of nineteen: live an ascetic life of wisdom. Augustine tried and failed to secure a connection with God apart from the life he had lived, but he had not yet seen truth is a person, Christ, the Word made flesh. The Christ he encounters in Book 8 will invite Augustine back into Augustine's own life—even as he invites him into a new one. Augustine confesses, "I could not even guess the mystery contained in the Word made flesh."[20]

In *Confessiones* 7, Augustine tries to relate to God as though he (Augustine) had never been born. God allows Augustine the conceit, but then offers Augustine deliverance into a life that is truly blessed. If we think we understand the life of spirit by imagining a womb from which we will never have to suffer parting, we have not begun to fathom the promise of spirit. If we think we understand the life of spirit by imagining a perfected life of flesh, a life of flesh without so many gaps and hesitations and grief—we do not understand spirit at all. We instead imagine the blessed life as a cosmic escape from human creatureliness. That paltry imagination for spirit is a temptation in *Confessiones* 7, and it is precisely what Augustine dramatizes in *De magistro*. We look to the divine Word to yield the clarity and intelligibility our own words lack, and we think that bodiless intelligibility is the best happy life for which we might hope. But Truth in person, Christ, whom Augustine will encounter in *Confessiones* 8, embodies another way of conceiving the perfection of life, both human and divine.

At the beginning of *Confessiones* 8, Augustine expresses his desire to be more stable in his concept of God, whom he encountered in *Confessiones* 7 as an immaterial Father of spirit. By the end of *Confessiones* 8, Augustine comes to feel most secured by the God who was born of a woman, the God who lived a human life. Encountering God in the person of Christ does not give Augustine greater willpower to overcome the apparent deficiencies of life in the flesh. Instead it delivers Augustine into a form of knowing and loving that persists through brokenness and darkness. Augustine's intimacy with God in *Confessiones* 8 is no cosmic meeting of the minds. It is more like a child's intimacy with a parent, or a lover's intimacy with a beloved. By evoking, at the moment of conversion, memories of two great loves—Augustine's love for the unnamed woman and his love for Adeodatus—God reminds Augustine that spirit and flesh need not always be antagonists. These memories are reminders of the plenitude of flesh and of the fruitful intimacy of spirit and flesh. The authority of Christ, appearing under the mediation of a child's voice, shows Augustine that life with God is life in the care of others. Intimacy delivers Augustine into the understanding and security he needs.

Much of *Confessiones* 8 records the turmoil in Augustine's soul as he moves toward an embrace of the life of Christ. For Augustine, conversion will mean a renunciation of his professional ambitions and a life of celibacy. He hears and is moved by the testimonies of others who have turned from big secular careers and betrothals to new lives of perfect surrender to God. He bitterly laments his own hesitation. His perception of truth is no longer uncertain, but some fear holds him back: "Yet I was still bound to the earth and refused to serve you, because I was just as scared to be set free from my baggage as I was to continue carrying it."[21] Augustine's fear here is of a piece with the memory that dragged him back from his vision of the immaterial God. Augustine both does and does not want to be free from his so-called baggage. It conserves some memory of belonging, some experience of intimacy. As he considers a conversion that, for him, would involve an irrevocable commitment to celibacy, it is no wonder losing this baggage might spark fear. Augustine is certain that surrender to God's love is preferable to succumbing to his lust, but a part of him worries how he will survive without his habitual ways of trying to care for his flesh.

Augustine's conversion may be precipitated by memories of intimacy, but intimacy is emphatically not Augustine's initial tactic for moving himself toward love of God, as we see in the beginning of *Confessiones* 8. After a conversation with Ponticianus, Augustine recalls using harsh language to force himself to follow his Master: "What did I not tell myself? What whip of argument did I not use to scourge my soul into following me, as I tried to follow you? It resisted and would not yield, but could find no excuse."[22]

Augustine's attempts to discipline himself into following the way of faith parallel his teachers' attempts to discipline the schoolboy Augustine into learning Greek: "I knew none of those words, and I was threatened with savage, terrifying punishments to make me learn them."[23] This harsh technique was ineffective at disciplining the child's mind into fruitful study of Greek, and it is similarly ineffective at disciplining the resistant soul. Though without excuse, Augustine's battered soul hangs back, terrified.

Perhaps Augustine evokes the memory of his entry into language as he is on the cusp of an embrace of a life of faith and celibacy to remind himself and his reader of the great difference between a knowledge (a) that is the result of abuse and self-discipline and (b) that flows out of security and love. Immediately after his account of his struggles with Greek, Augustine warmly recollects his initiation into his Latin tongue: "I certainly did not know any Latin as an infant, but I learned by paying attention, without any fear or suffering, amid nurses who spoiled me, and laughter, joking, and the fun of playing around."[24] He learned Latin without pressure or threat of punishment, amid caresses and laughter, in the care of those who loved him. As the moment of his conversion nears, why does Augustine evoke this traumatic scourging of himself as a small boy—and its twin memory of a more pleasurable, playful entry into speech? The conjunction suggests that any fluency the adult Augustine might develop with the Word of God will come not through greater self-discipline, but by knowing himself to be a child, already known and loved.

As Augustine struggles to will what he does and does not want, he is presented with a curious sight: the "pure, dignified figure of Continence" (*conf.* 8.11.27). Lady Continence appears to Augustine, stretching out her hands to show many good examples for him to follow. She is the mother of a multitude of children, joys born of her consort with the Lord. The serene and cheerful lady reminds Augustine that the children she presents to him did not receive their joys by their own resources, but as a gift. She enjoins him to quit relying on himself and to cast himself on God, leaping with a child's confidence that the arms of his father will catch him: "Cast yourself on him. Do not be afraid. We will not abandon you and let you fall."[25] Continence is presented not as the achievement of a less divided will but as the gift of a loving parent. Lady Continence invites Augustine to become like a child, venturing forth on trust rather than on the strength of mature self-discipline. Augustine, still giving an ear to vanities, blushes with embarrassment at the Lady's invitation.

Augustine's blush may signal his sharp awareness of his personal relationship to Lady Continence's life of celibacy. When Augustine and Monica sent away the mother of Adeodatus, she promised a life of continence, vowing never to know another man (*conf.* 6.15.25). Though profoundly wounded by their separation, Augustine found himself unable to follow her example. Instead he took a stopgap mistress while he waited for a third woman, his betrothed, to come of age. This measure did not heal Augustine's wound, which continued to fester (*conf.* 6.15.25). Augustine was then unable to imitate the vow made by his partner, but as he moves toward conversion, the issue of celibacy comes to the fore again.

Lady Continence is arguably a double for Augustine's unnamed partner, the mother of Adeodatus.[26] Augustine's conversion is precipitated by hearing the conversion stories of several men: Victorinus, who gave up his career in rhetoric, and some minor administrative officers, who renounced not just their careers but also their conjugal life with their fiancées. These male examples of continence appeal to Augustine, but leave him frustrated and unable to act. Lady Continence brings Augustine to a climax of grief and tears. The penultimate invitation to continence, haunted by the memory of the unnamed woman, perhaps carries with it a promise of intimacy restored. For Augustine, celibacy will not take him further from the intimacy he once knew with the mother of his child. Such a vow is the only way Augustine can be close to his partner again. He will share in her commitment to a life of celibacy. Of course, that intimacy is far from the forms of intimacy they once knew. But the fact that the invitation to continence comes not from himself nor from another man but from a woman—a fruitful mother—eases Augustine's interior struggle. Augustine experienced, sometimes, good care for his flesh. His relationship with the unnamed woman was not merely a pact of lust.[27] It was a place of intimate belonging in their shared life and of fruitfulness in the form of their child. Those goods need not be lost in Augustine's turn to Christ. Embracing the life of Christ is a way of embracing the goodness of Augustine's love for the unnamed woman and the admittedly incomplete goodness of the life Augustine had already been living. If Lady Continence evokes the unnamed woman, Augustine can be assured that a turn to Christ could be a turn toward care for his flesh, and a turn away from unsatisfying ways of trying to shut up his desire. Christ does not call Augustine from intimacy to greater discipline of his needy flesh. Instead Christ and Lady Continence invite Augustine to recover a lost intimacy.

Augustine withdraws from the presence of his friend Alypius to give himself over to weeping. He grieves his wretchedness and makes a sacrifice of tears to his Lord. He begs God not to remember his sins, sins by which he feels himself held as prisoner. No longer does Augustine beg to be given "chastity and continence—but not yet" (*conf.* 8.7.17). Instead, he feels that even tomorrow is too long to wait to embrace a life of continence. He desires an end to his depravity, not just today, but in the very hour in which he speaks. The choking words, the flood of tears, the dramatic gestures—withdrawing from his companion and throwing himself to the ground under a fig tree—show Augustine has come to a crisis point. He wants to be rid of his wretchedness. He wants to imitate the feminine model of continence he has seen.

Augustine's tears are checked by the voice of a child who calls *tolle, lege*, chanting as though playing some sort of game, though not a game Augustine knows (*conf.* 8.12.29). Augustine takes the voice to be divinely authoritative, and he obeys. In imitation of those whose stories he had heard, Augustine turns to a book that happens to be lying nearby (a volume of Paul), and he flips it open at random. The first verse his eyes fall upon speaks directly to him (*conf.* 8.12.29; Chadwick trans.): "Not in riots and drunken parties, not in eroticism and indecencies, not in strife and rivalry, but put on the Lord Jesus Christ and make no provision for the flesh in its lusts."[28] Augustine has neither need nor desire to read one word more. At the end of the verse, the dark shades of doubt (*dubitationis tenebrae*) have been chased off by the light of security (*luce securitatis*; *conf.* 8.12.29).

At first blush, it is not obvious why this specific verse brings Augustine more illumination. The verse tells Augustine to put on the Lord Jesus Christ and stop engaging in immorality. It is unclear why reading that verse would help Augustine replace his impotent will with Christ's firmer one. If the end of the story is that God gifts Augustine with divine power to restrain his sexual desire and enter into divine life, Augustine sounds like a revert to Manichaeism, possessing the power to effect a conversion from flesh to spirit. It is not hard to imagine Augustine hearing that verse from

Romans and remaining unmoved—or taking it as further indictment of his belated conversion.

The framing of the passage makes all the difference. Augustine reads it at the prompting of a child's voice.[29] Thus the verse comes to Augustine in the context of a memory of childhood (both his own and that of his son) and in the context of a memory of his love for his unnamed partner. All are memories of the fullness and beauty of his life in the flesh and of his life as a creature, both child and parent. They are memories of intimacy. As he shared a life with those two beloved ones, Augustine found his body a rich and expressive palette for knowing and relating to them. His body did not preclude knowledge in these relationships, but was part of how he was able to know and express his love for these two. The evocation of the memories of Augustine's son and partner remind him that the most profound forms of intelligibility are engendered by love.

This child's voice does not aim at persuading Augustine of some fact. It does not tell him that he is sinful or that he has misunderstood a particular point of theology or metaphysics. In fact, it communicates very little by way of content. It merely gives a directive that happens to prove fruitful. More importantly, it is evocative, reminding Augustine of a good parent's love for his child. The voice hints that Augustine need not restore a lost intimacy before God will speak to him. The intimacy is lost only insofar as it has been unacknowledged, or even resisted by Augustine. Augustine tried and failed to make himself perfect. The voice of the child reminds Augustine that he is already a son of his divine Father. The matrix of their intimacy is not conditional on his perfection. God hopes Augustine might find a way to live not out of an adult sense of mastery but out of a child-like trust of connectedness. Augustine wants to learn the difference between presumption and confession (*conf.* 7.20.26). Which is the greater presumption: to imagine that a father would welcome back his suffering son, or to think he would not?

Augustine had already found in *Confessiones* 7 that he cannot find spirit simply by escaping his flesh and its disposition to seek satisfaction in other flesh. Christ gives no power for that project. The way Augustine had been trying to care for his flesh had been life-denying, dominated by a sense of the neediness of his flesh. Wetzel's translation of Paul's words highlights this: "No more wild parties and drunken fits, bedroom antics and indecencies, rivalries and wrangling; just put on Jesus Christ, your master, and don't look to lusts to care for your flesh."[30] Augustine tried to care for his flesh, to preserve it, by satisfying his lust, but this was a losing strategy. Wetzel sums up the revelation: "lusts . . . do not parent flesh."[31] Perhaps such sexual torment as Augustine suffered was a symptom, not the cause of Augustine's disease. Living out of a sense of the poverty of his life in the flesh, he moved toward such relief as he could find. His lust kept him attuned to his sense of lack, a lack reinforced with each passing satisfaction. He served desires that presupposed a poverty of flesh and continued to suffer from a sense of that poverty. It is no wonder Augustine was tempted to imagine spirit as flesh without lack—as perfect connection, perfect clarity, perfect illumination. But that is not the intimacy into which Christ, the Word, invites Augustine.

Christ invites Augustine into a new way in the flesh: not a way of stability nor a way of remaining unmoved but a way that recalls plenitude and connection. Wetzel writes, "Augustine's conversion is not from lust to self-restraint. It is from murky self-preoccupation to the precise tension of a life consciously lived with others."[32] The truest love of creatures draws Augustine into intimacy with both creatures and Creator. God reminds Augustine that his human life is the very life through which he has learned to love God. Augustine's love of God finally comes not out of a sense of escape, but out of recollection of the beauty of the life Augustine had already been living. Moved by memory, Augustine is recalled to intimacy, with his Creator and with the creatures he loves: partner, child, friends. Augustine does not receive the stability he sought. Instead, he is given the light of security. He will still suffer change, still be moved, but all that will occur within the security a child feels within the bonds of a good parent's love.

Augustine comes to feel most secured by the lordship of Christ, one who was intimate with the flesh and who knew flesh, but without Augustine's apparent sense of deficiency. If Jesus Christ is going to be lord over Augustine's flesh, he will not cut Augustine off from his fleshly attachments. Instead Christ's authority draws Augustine out of the motherless womb of *Confessiones* 7 and into a life and flesh in the care of others. If Christ's lordship over Augustine's body will be anything like his lordship over his own, it will look like a willingness to let himself be nurtured— to know the touch of women and men, and to know connection through both pleasure and woundedness. One can live a life born of a woman without that life being corrupt at its root. Christ loved that life, desired it, even as his spirit Father desired his mortal mother. Christ did not make his way in the world by trying to escape his flesh. Instead he allowed himself to be intimate with creation. He continues to give his flesh to the care of others precisely because he cares about it.

For parent and child, no life is fully one's own. Life is not something one can give oneself.[33] It breathes and rests in the care of others. In *Confessiones* 8, Augustine shows his readers that life in the care of God is life in the care of others. This is true both for him and, paradigmatically, for Christ. This God is a son, one who lived a human life in the care and under the authority of others.[34] He does not care for himself, raise himself, and provide for himself. He does not map out the terms of his own life and insist that others buy into the story he tells. Instead he—God himself—lives a life the meaning of which is told and shaped by the love and care of others. The evocation of the lordship of Christ, couched in the memories of Augustine's bonds with others he had loved, reminds Augustine that he need not try to speak beyond the bonds of the life he had already been living. That life gives Augustine's words such meanings as they have.

Augustine's conversion is no turn toward some private inward space where he and God can know each other, free from the hang-ups and confusions of ordinary, time-bound life. Throughout *Confessiones* 8, Augustine is drawn toward Christ through imitation, giving himself into the care and better judgment of others. Augustine moves toward God not through a series of deductions, nor through summoning his inner strength. He moves toward God through memory and by attending more closely to his own life. When Augustine tried to find his way to God guided largely by his inner resources, he was like one unborn, one not yet existing. But when he allows himself to recall and acknowledge his connection to Adeodatus and to the boy's mother, Augustine is drawn not toward an impossible ideal but toward a form of life. His conversion is not a matter of achievement but a matter of resting in the wisdom of those he knows and loves most intimately.

Augustine rushes out of the garden so that he might share with his mother the news of his embrace of faith and celibacy (*conf.* 8.12.30). The departure from the courtyard dramatically represents Augustine's departure from the womb. Having heard the voice of a child, Augustine is born again. In drawing near to his mother, Augustine hints that his rebirth is not an undoing of his first birth into his body. He suggests his knowledge of God comes not despite but through his life as a creature. Augustine may still have regrets over his lost years and his lamentably late love of God, but the voice of the child and the feminine figure of Continence serve to remind Augustine that his very aspiration to love God more fully is itself a fruit of his past.

God does not ask Augustine to resolve some contradiction between knowing spirit and needy flesh to be beloved of his Father. There is no such contradiction for God the Father, who desires and loves mortal life. And there is no such contradiction for Jesus Christ, whose one life was both divine and human. Augustine is reminded that the intimacy of a life shared with another is the very ground and nourishment of understanding. He moves toward the beata vita by embracing precisely those human attachments he was tempted to shed. Christ tells us that the only way into the kingdom is to become like a child, and that demands birth. That birth—a birth back into life with others—may involve a suffering dark as death, but the alternative is utterly lifeless.

Augustine's invocation of the beata vita in *De magistro* comes right in the middle of the unfolding argument for the thesis that we talk to inform and the involved discussion of signification. He tells Adeodatus, "But if I said there is a happy and eternal life to which I hope God—our guide, who is Truth itself—might lead us in stages accommodated to our uncertain steps, then I'm afraid I might seem ridiculous, because I started off with a consideration not of the things signified, but of signs."[35] He suggests that their conversation is preparing them for and even birthing them into that life. Because the dialogue is an unfolding conversation rather than a treatise, the image of birth presented can be read in different ways. Father and son work out what they mean together. My own reading of the parturition passage in *De magistro* is ambivalent. I want to say both that the parturition passage challenges the thesis that we talk to inform, but also that the passage reflects an attachment to that thesis. That is to say, the parturition image can be read as consonant with the talking-to-inform thesis, but it also draws father and son into richer possibilities.

I begin with the flatter reading—the one that hears the image as reflective of the talking-to-inform thesis. The parturition passage is marked by a curious omission. Augustine describes two men (and one divine Father) trying to give birth to a life. Augustine proposes the image of a birth into something wonderful but coming out of nothing or out of no one. As father and son speak of birth and happiness, it would be altogether natural to acknowledge the memory of the beloved mother of Adeodatus. Even faced with an image of this woman—his son, in whom Augustine must have seen traces of her features and gestures—and even while talking about himself and his son being birthed into new life, Augustine has no word to speak of her.

Augustine invites his son into a motherless birth. Because they are committed, at this point in the conversation, to the thesis that we talk to inform, they speak of life as something achieved rather than given. Perhaps Augustine and Adeodatus will serve as midwives to each other. But it sounds more like each is going to enjoy this birth on the strength of his training and his limbering-up exercises. This is a far cry from ordinary, nonmetaphorical births wherein a mother gifts a child with life. In fact, the metaphor of birth seems misplaced here. What Augustine describes is no event of deliverance. What is missing in this passage is a strong sense of life as something that is given. Missing as well is a robust sense of life—mortal, earthly, human, finite life.

In this way, the passage is an image of what it is to talk to inform: when we talk to inform, life is something we have to give ourselves. Or when we talk to inform, life is something we have to engineer for ourselves. That way of putting it highlights that such a life and birth have little to do with incarnation, with being constituted by life with and from others, in time and history. When Augustine describes how he and his son will make their way into the happy life, he sounds like an unborn homunculus. A fetal adult strategizes about how to get born into the world, blind to the fact that the walls that seem to confine him are both the source of his life and the site for his deliverance. When we try to parent our own beata vita, we act like orphaned children of God, pulling ourselves out of the darkness and into existence.

When we speak to inform, we imagine our meanings are fully available to our minds and communication is a matter of teaching internally articulated meanings to those outside us. In *Confessiones* 1, Augustine uses the metaphor of birth to describe his verbal expression of his inner life: "My own heart urged me to deliver what I had conceived, which would have been impossible without all those words I had learned—not from teachers, but from those with whom I spoke and in whose ears I completed the parturition of what I was thinking."[36] If we are each stuck inside ourselves, our lives are basically closed off to those in other bodies, and the fact of our incarnation seems to be an impediment to speaking well with each other. It seems like our shabby signs signal across an unnavigable distance. But to accept that framing of the problem is already to have lost the game, as Augustine knows. Mind and world, language and flesh, are not dualisms requiring a calculated effort of reconnection. They are in fact already bound together in our ordinary life with language, as Augustine shows us. The conversation in *De magistro* is innocent of the angst of separation. In *De magistro*, father and son speak easily together. The lives they have lived shape what they mean together, and their relationship carries them through the moments of confusion and misapprehension.

In the *Confessiones* 1 image, it is the interlocutors' thoughts and words that are getting born. But in Augustine's birthing metaphor in *De magistro*, the interlocutors are themselves being born. This image is an image of transformation, which is why I say my reading of it is ambivalent. The ambivalence is built right into the image. As I noted earlier, the image reflects a strange contraction of language—the desire to speak only to inform. But contraction and constriction are inseparable here from parturition. The one who is yet unborn has no idea what it will mean to be born. It is an unanticipatable event. His ways of talking about it cannot but be beholden to old forms and understandings.

The working through of the temptation to think that we talk only to inform one another—and the contracted imagination for spirit and interiority that accompanies that conviction—is precisely what moves us into knowledge and love of God—and love of that life we share with others. We are tempted to contract the meaning of our words—to suggest that they serve only to inform, across the distance from one embodied mind to another. Augustine knows that we often try to cling to that contraction—to live with it and in it, permanently, instead of letting ourselves be delivered out of our cramped way with words. Yet our problematic contraction of meaning may, over time, draw us out into the heat and light of the beata vita, a place where we can live. The beata vita is not what we imagine from our vantage within that strained and narrowed approach to meaning where we work to get a fix on words and minds. Augustine ushers us through that contraction and into deliverance into a life most blessed.

Augustine tells Adeodatus that their conversation is an exercise, one that will prepare them to love the beata vita: "Forgive me, then, this playful prelude. It's not for the sake of mere amusement, but to exercise our mental strength and attention, to prepare us not just to withstand but to love the warmth and light of that place where the happy life is found."[37] Their conversation cannot spell out what exactly that life will be, only that it will be beata. The conversation promises to help father and son love and enjoy that life, but Augustine takes the exercises to be propaedeutic, a spiritual exercise to prepare them for a hope beyond all expectation. As Augustine makes clear in *Confessiones* 7 and 8, the birth into the beata vita is not an escape from human life and human knowing. The birth for which father and son hope is a form of deliverance into life with others and with God. We are already more connected than we know. That is the life most blessed.

CHAPTER FIVE

MOTHER OF THE WORD

In part 1, we examined the temptation to think that words serve primarily to inform others, and we considered the temptation to think that Christ, the inner teacher, is a deus ex machina, an outworking of a divine Father's attempts to inform our minds. Irigaray painted the portrait of that teacher-informer in her mythic retellings of the births of Dionysus, Apollo, and Christ, where each in his own way served as an image for talking to inform. *De magistro* hints at the connection between the desire to inform and a motherless birth. But Irigaray also reminds us the story of Christ can be told differently, with attention to the mutual desire between spirit and flesh. That story is the subject of this chapter, and it prepares us for a detailed examination of Augustine's account of the inner teacher in the next chapter.

Augustine calls the inner teacher *Christ*, not *the Word*, as one might expect in a dialogue about words.[1] The image is underdetermined, perhaps intentionally so. Augustine does not spell out the richness of what it means to have a divine presence within. Likewise, he proposes that conversation is part of being birthed into the blessed life, life with God, but he does not tease out the implications of his provocative metaphor. In short, he invokes the divine, but does not nail down what it means. How could he? By way of response to Augustine's evocative image, my purpose in this chapter is to put some flesh on it. I do not mean to suggest that Augustine's account was inadequate or missing pieces. Since he suggests that meaning emerges not from words alone but from the dynamic between interlocutors, I propose to respond to Augustine's text by playing with his image of the inner teacher.

Augustine encourages his son to listen to the inner teacher. Though Augustine does not make the point, Mary, the mother of God, arguably knew better than anyone how to listen to the Christ within. If we want to know how to learn from and love Christ, we would do well to look at how his mother related to him. She received a Word at the Annunciation, and she birthed that Word into the world. The Word Mary receives is not merely the Father's best idea, but a living, incarnate being who grows up over and in time. She models for us how to parent words in others and in ourselves. Therefore I turn now to Irigaray's retelling of Mary's story in *Marine Lover*. Through her portrait of Mary, her divine partner, and her infant Word, we can deepen our understanding of the essential connection between Word and life.

Irigaray also expands our imagination for why the divine Father speaks. What could a god have to say to humans? Augustine began the dialogue by asking Adeodatus what we want when we speak with one another. Through his turn to Christ, the inner teacher, in *De magistro*, we are invited to reflect on why God the Father and Christ his son speak with us. Irigaray proposes the Father is moved to speak by love and by desire. She suggests that we do not speak to ventriloquize the teaching of our divine Father, and she reminds us of the divine Father's affection for mortal life. This Father seems to have no interest in controlling the order of signification. He seems more interested in eliciting attention and love. The Word comes to life in the context of intimacy. He is given life out of what poet Scott Cairns calls the mutual obsession of spirit and flesh.[2] Irigaray reminds her reader that incarnate life is no obstacle to meaning and fulfillment. It is the context within which words come to life.

In her retelling of the Christian myth, Irigaray imagines that the relation between gods and human beings began not with indifference or disdain but with connection. Irigaray says the presence of God felt by Adam and Eve in the garden was indistinct from their very selves. Perhaps the myth of earthly paradise, suggests Irigaray, is Eve's memorial to the existence she once knew, existence in God. In that existence, man and woman shared heaven and earth. They were unsheltered, uncovered, naked. The divine was not opposed to them nor distinct from them. God walked with them in the cool of the evening. "He was in them as they were in him."³ When the divine was in the midst of and between man and woman, it was the very center of their attraction. They lived without "store of 'suprasensory' knowledge to separate them from the innocence of fleshly communion."⁴

The fall interrupted that basic intimacy. On Irigaray's telling, the first couple's banishment occurred when the real, material presence of God came to be felt to be something *apart* from human beings. They took themselves to be apart from God, and God became distant, a model to be imitated. The first couple identified that difference between them and God as rooted in their bodily existence. The first couple asserted that the body is not of God, and God acquiesced to their insistence. For their punishment, they were thrown out into guilty desires and pains of the flesh, and they learned to take those desires and pains to be their own, what set them apart from the divine. In this way, evil, sin, suffering, and redemption arose, writes Irigaray.⁵ Once the eyes of Adam and Eve were opened, showing them what they took to be the shame of their bodies and the appeal of the beyond, all women and men began to long for redemption. "The earth becomes a great deportation camp, where men await celestial redemption."⁶ The earth became something to escape, to get beyond. Mortals could work toward that escape by being obedient and faithful, not to mortal life, but to the eternal beyond.

Yet, after the exile from Eden, God still allowed himself to be encountered in the senses—by Abraham, Hagar, Sarai, Jacob, and Moses. God did not fully withdraw into heaven, and he left his mark on the body of those men who encountered him. To those who came later, God's presence would be conveyed through a law inscribed on stone tablets. By the time he gives the law, God only allows himself to be seen from the back while Moses—incarnated, mortal, and sexed as he is—hides in the crevice of a rock. The law is the Word of God made *writing*. God does not touch, but speaks in stone words that are given over to commentators and translators. The will of God is impassable, words carved in stone. God's presence is taken to be most fully realized in the law, bestowed from on high and written in stone. This stony word, a codified law, becomes the Word of God, and, on Irigaray's telling, commandments, preaching, temples, priests all conspire to deaden the life incarnate, the life that is intimate and near. It is not long before the fighting begins over who possesses the true God, over who knows him as he is. The signs in stone are contested, the mantle of their glory contested. The fight for power produces bloodshed again and again.

Though God is present in mineral-inscribed law, in what is least porous, Scripture also maintains that God is present in a guiding cloud, in what is most porous. So too, in the ark of the covenant, his presence is manifest in the empty, airy between. In this emptiness, Irigaray suggests, his advent is prepared.[7] In the midst of fights over dead letters, etched in stone, he returns in an unexpected place, a living place, and a place of vulnerability: the womb of a virgin. Perhaps Mary is the only one who still knows—or hopes—that the divine might maintain some connection with a life in time, a life in flesh. "The presence that had been buried and paralyzed in the text of the law is made flesh once more in the body of a woman, guardian of the spirit of the divine life."[8] Mary gives living flesh to the Word she apprehends.

The intimacy between God and human beings is recovered through attention—Mary's to God, and God's to Mary. Their intimacy is engendered not by the divine Father's attempts to inform, but by his expression of love in which he invites her to parent a child with him, to bring a Word to life with him. This God gazes not only on eternity but also on the beauty of a mortal woman. Likewise, Mary's careful attention and delicate sensitivity are the conditions for the renewed intimacy between God and human beings. In the message of the angel, Mary hears something more than simply the will of the Father. Mary does not just simply receive the Word from God. Rather she draws it forth, begetting that Word in consort with the Father. She engenders her word out of communion with the "*cosmos* which she lives in and which lives in her, and shelters in her."[9] She is attuned to the voice of God, and the child comes through that attunement. The Word she sends forth is spoken out of faithful attention to both heaven and earth. It comes to life, comes forth, through the attentive love of both the Father and the Mother.

In Mary, the Word becomes flesh. For her, the Word is not simply the best possible *idea*, but something intimate, interior, and responsive to her most fundamental desires as an embodied soul. In depictions of the Annunciation, Mary is sometimes shown with a book in hand or open on her lap. She first encounters the Word of God as words in written form, perhaps reading the prophecy in Isaiah that a virgin will give birth to a child. In the artist Simone Martini's rendering of the scene, Mary is touched not with a typical shaft of light from heaven but with a golden shaft of words sent from the angel's mouth toward her ear: "*Ave gratia plena dominus tecum.* / Hail woman full of grace, the Lord is with you."[10] These artistic representations suggest Mary is impregnated by the words she hears—impregnated by and with the Word of God. She is not indifferent to what she reads and hears. She cannot keep it at a distance. She takes in the words and brings them to life. Her response is anything but abstracted or disinterested. It is made up of her very flesh. Not merely a recipient or receptacle for the divine Word, she gives that Word life.

This is a world away from the ideal communication we imagined (in part 1) to consist of passing thoughts from mind to mind in contemplation of what is most abstract, most exalted, and most sublime. The meaning of God's Word, then, is not fully controlled by the Father. God surrenders his own Word to Mary and to humankind. God does not fix the meaning of his Word in Mary; he does not obliterate her humanity through expression of his fully determinate will. Mary is not just receptive and passive, not just a chalice into which the love of the Father overflows. Her response is creative, full of life and grace. God invites her to co-create and co-parent the Word with Himself, within her womb, household, and culture. This Word has not just a father, but a mother too.

The messenger knew his message would frighten, and he exhorts her not to fear. The Lord is near, is with you. What could such a thing mean to a virgin young woman? Surely she could little imagine why or how she had found this favor of divine attention. Perhaps this is why so many depictions of the Annunciation show Mary shrinking back, an adolescent girl trying to shirk her very skin, from within a body that hardly seems hers. When the angel arrives, she cannot understand what is wanted, cannot understand why she is wanted, why she is sought. Can she abide the thought that the Lord is with her? Can she acknowledge that she is with the Lord? Is intimacy with the divine something to be countenanced, or must she avert her gaze? The question pondered by the mother of all the living (Mary's struggle just as Eve's): is desire outside of and foreign to the Father-God?

Mary's Word is given life through her love with the Father. What sort of love is it? I think here of the Scott Cairns poem "Loves: Magdalen's

Epistle," in which Magdalen, a woman "recalled for having won a touch /
of favor from the one we call / the son of man," exhorts her reader not to
forget "the very issue which / induced the Christ to take on flesh."[11] Cairns's
Magdalene suggests the inducement was not pity nor condescension, but
desire. He did not come to her to realize some cosmic backup plan for re-
storing a fallen world nor to make a show of expressing his sovereign will.
Instead, Magdalene explains, God came with love, love for all humankind
in the form of love for one particular woman. Cairns's Magdalene describes
Christ: "I have looked long / into the trouble of his face, / and met, in that
intersection, / the sacred place—where body / and spirit both abide, both
yield, / in mutual obsession."[12] It is easy to believe that the body is obsessed
with the spirit. The body, subject to unruly desires and weakness, would
surely desire the greater wisdom that the spirit seems to offer. Yet the story
of the Annunciation draws us toward the poet's more radical point—that
the body could attract the spirit's notice and that a particular body could
be the spirit's obsession. Such an insight might require in us a rethinking
of the very nature of spirit, the very nature of the holy, and the promise
of redemption.

The coming of God's Word to Mary is the advent of her darkness. She
is promised a great son, a ruler with a share in immortal life. But what she
is given looks to all the world like a curse: an illegitimate pregnancy with
an absent father, a pregnancy that raised questions about her continued
relationship with her betrothed, the very present and real Joseph. Were she
to see further into the future, she might have found little consolation: she
was to be the mother of a murdered son who would die in relative obscu-
rity, despite his grandiose pronouncements and promises to his small following. The angel announced God's desire to share a life with her, but she
can have no fully formed sense of what this means. What the divine messenger brings is supposed to be *something*, but, in Mary's mind and in her
body, whatever it is tends toward formlessness. She may have wondered
whether it was anything at all.

When we think we speak only to inform, we valorize the clear and
determinate ways of speaking that seem to make it easier to accomplish
that goal. This amounts to stripping the life out of our words. But Mary,
full of grace, offers her hope to us: that a word lacking full determinacy
may be good and life-giving. Mary shows us that darkness and opacity do

not always signal death, but are instead sometimes part of being delivered into life. The divine Word is sometimes hidden, sometimes dark, even as it promises to give life abundant. As she gestates her word, waiting for it to take shape, Mary waits in darkness. "I said to my soul, be still, and let the dark come upon you / Which shall be the darkness of God."[13] She waits out of a sense that inarticulacy is not always a signal of emptiness. Her embryonic word is indistinct, but it is to her not nothing; that word is a *promise* of life. The life of Mary and her son, the Word, suggests that risk, sorrow, and darkness are intrinsic to the divine life, not just the pitiable contribution of a shabby world. Mary dares to hope that the darkness was not outside God, not a signal of her being forsaken. Advent is a period of waiting, and Mary lives the virtue of hope. But hers is a hope beyond any determinate expectation. "I said to my soul, be still, and wait without hope / For hope would be hope for the wrong thing."[14] Mary trusts that indeterminacy is not always a manifestation of lack, but holds the promise of fecundity. Mary trusts that a thing lacking full determination may be good.

This darkness, the darkness of what is not comprehensively articulated— a darkness that looks like empty blackness—is precisely what we try to flee when we talk only to inform. The temptation is to try to illuminate that darkness by drawing our nascent sense into the light of articulacy. We try to make our words more articulate, more exact, less tethered to ourselves, more sublime. But perversely, in doing so, we sever the cord that gives our words life. If the demand for articulacy is ahead of time, our word may arrive stillborn or aborted, taken too soon from the place of its gestation for it to be able to live and breathe in the world. Our hasty attempt to prove that something is living or productive may disrupt the fragile life that had begun.

For Mary, the Word is just not something she can grasp. There is no getting a fix on meaning, no shutting down other possibilities of saying, hearing, and knowing proliferating senses. In Mary, the Word becomes. The vitality of the Word means it is given to life in many forms. It/He will live a life independent of his mother's control or sovereignty. Mary and her divine consort risk letting their issue make his own way in the world, walking and wandering at will. The life her Word lives, both within and without her, outstrips any possibility of predicting or imagining it in advance. A Word that grows, that lives, that breathes—that becomes— must be multiple, proliferating in meanings wherever it finds itself. Mary's example invites us to find ease with the becoming of our own words, to welcome the way they bloom and flower, outstripping full comprehension and articulation.

Mary demonstrates the fruitful dynamic that exists not just between divine and human speakers but between human interlocutors too. Full of anxious joy, Mary rushes to visit her cousin Elizabeth. At the Annunciation, the angel brings a message promising new life to Mary, and now Mary's message draws forth evidence of new life within Elizabeth. When Mary greets Elizabeth, the infant life quickens within the woman who was called barren. In that moment, Mary comes to know the effect her word might have on another. This Word that Mary cannot comprehend and cannot yet share because it is still latent within her, nonetheless causes life to stir within another. Here is a promise that her Word is not just for her, but may be vitalizing to others who encounter her. Mary's Word—and the potential of Mary's Word—gave joy to one who loved her. Perhaps this moment gave comfort to Mary—deepening her confidence in the potential of what she had been given—and was a consolation to her during those further months when her Word would remain hidden and opaque to her.

One Word remains hidden in Mary's encounter with Elizabeth, for it is still too much to let go—too much and too little, tiny and unformed as it is. But Mary does have something at heart to say. Responding to the words of Elizabeth, "Blessed art thou among women, and blessed is the fruit of thy womb," Mary speaks her confidence that she is in fact blessed, that she will be called blessed by all who live after her. In this scene, Mary finds more than the few, timid words she musters in reply to the angelic messenger. As she celebrates with Elizabeth, Mary testifies to her joy and to the powerful and merciful exploits of her God; her words flow forth in the easy way they so often do between intimates. Once again, words are birthed in love, and Mary speaks beyond herself. Playing on Elizabeth's comment that Mary is blessed, the younger woman gushes that all generations will call her blessed. In this way she spoke more than she, limited in time and history, could have known. It is tempting to want our voices to be sure, to speak only out of certain knowledge. Yet Mary's example reminds us that speaking sometimes moves us forward into understanding. Perhaps we who love wisdom might allow ourselves to speak from the darkness or wilderness, speak out of wonder, affection, desire, dissolution. Perhaps we might speak out of advent rather than fulfillment.

The situation with Elizabeth's husband, Zachariah, is quite different. It is a kind of counterexample, an instance of refusing to listen to the inner teacher and refusing to trust in the slow unfolding of the meanings of words. When an angel of the Lord arrives in the sanctuary of the Lord to share the news of his elderly wife's pregnancy with Zachariah, the old man is shocked and doubtful. He asks how he can know the angelic message is true, and he explains why it is unlikely to be true. Zachariah, though he is physically proximate to the divine (in the Holy Place), demands a better, more certain annunciation. He is, in fact, receiving a direct answer to his prayer for the repentance of the people of Israel. He is told his own child will turn the hearts of many to God. But he does not allow the context of the message to count. If he had acknowledged the source and context of the words, he would have recognized them as trustworthy, not duplicitous or empty.

Insofar as we approach them with a critical, skeptical eye and insofar as we insist that they cannot have any power or life that outstrips our comprehension and power, our words are dumb. Skeptical Zachariah quickly finds himself wordless. After he rejects the new life on offer, God strikes him dumb. Both Mary and Zachariah are offered new life. The one who is resistant is left dumb, while the other, curiously attuned to the divine overture, is filled with speech and joyfully responds to the bizarre divine message at the Annunciation with words of her own and with a son, a new life of her own. Once Elizabeth and Zachariah's child finally arrives, however, he is named by his father. And once the little child is present in their midst, the father Zachariah is given words of his own, and he gives full voice to his joy.

Over nine months, Mary is faithful to the Word growing within her. She takes a Word from another, but she also makes it her own, nurturing it and gestating it in her own body. That Word is her intimate, but it is also her issue. Mary's encounter with the Word issues forth a voice of her own. The Word enters into her, and her body enters into speaking. She too, by speaking, lives. She, by speaking her word, incarnates the divine. Her saying transfigures her, pulls her forth from the walls of her death. We can hear in Mary's voice the possibility of a saying that does not drain bodies of life and animation, does not deaden them or neutralize them with a language of abstract universality.[15] This saying is not a dull repetition or mimicry of a lifeless Truth. Language can be a site of deliverance, into life and out of the confined and restricted sense of meaning to which we cling.

What does it mean that the Word is not just the *idea* of the Father-God but is in fact *incarnate*? It cannot mean that the Word was spoken once and for all as a universally applicable paradigm; the Word cannot be so divorced from the world of becoming.[16] The incarnation of the Word of the Father cannot be dependent on a language always and everywhere the same; the incarnate Word is not a static Truth fully revealed and now subject only to decoding by a clique of experts. This faithfulness of the Word to the flesh might cause us to rethink our sense of what language is and what words are. Irigaray writes, "Does the 'death of God' not mean, therefore, the end of the security lodged with, of the credit accorded to, those who thus suspend meaning in the letter? Those who immobilize life in something that is merely the trace of life?"[17] When we speak, we can have no certainty that meaning is located once and for all in an eternal realm of logic that our words aim to capture. Unlike Zeus, the Christian Father-God is no longer the only source of the meaning of the Word. The words Zeus sent were ghostly, otherworldly, and undead. Christ, the Word, has sometimes been taken to be one of these stillborn children, but Irigaray reinvigorates his image with her insistence that his life in the flesh is neither illusion nor punishing exile from the house of his Father. She resists any attempts to deaden his life by making him into an idea, accessible to all in the very same way, despite distances of time, space, and intimacy.

This divine presence returns to earth, "conceived and born by an attentive love,"[18] and he lives out of that love. Christ lives beyond the bounds of law, formula, and text. These modes of mediation place him at a distance; they make the kingdom of God the object only of nostalgia or expectation. Christ shows that the kingdom of God can be here and now, and he incarnates a new way of life, one not characterized by saying no.[19] Those who interpret Christ as a "timid or morbid adolescent, too paralyzed to realize his desires, always attentive to his Father's edicts, executing the Father's wishes even to the point of accepting the passion and the Father's desertion as the price of such fidelity"[20] have misunderstood the coming of the Word. Those who glorify the son of man only for his abstinence and for his death and resurrection, those who cannot see that his very presence in the flesh was a divine manifestation, and those who believe the kingdom of heaven is present only insofar as the flesh is stripped away—all such people have forgotten who they are. They beg to enter eternity, but they are already dead to time and to becoming. What more could they imagine eternity to be?

We struggle to admit that our words become. We hide from ourselves the knowledge that our words are created. We pretend our words drop from heaven, fully formed (and armed), ready to be pressed into service expressing thoughts. We suspect words signify truly only insofar as they transcend creation, allowing our minds to hook up with something real, eternal, and perfect. And we may be ashamed by our mundane words (the only words we have), by words that so obviously come from somewhere and from someone. Our knowledge that the words we speak are not sublime makes us worry they can only disappoint. They sound too pedestrian to signify anything worthy.

But the story of the nativity of Mary's Word tells us that her Word—the paradigmatic Word—is born. In a stable, he arrives amid muck and manure, impurity and stench. He is laid to rest in a manger, where animals had licked up their grain. Christ, the Word, does not hold himself apart from creation. He arrives as an infant, one who is still becoming, one who is vulnerable and weak. He is given to the care of another. As he grows, he is formed by his mother—and by all mortals who will know, love, hate, or live indifferently to him. Why does the divine Father take such a risk? The Word is so vulnerable to the world that it ends up losing its life, shedding its blood.

How could we understand a Word having a mother? The story of Christ as given in the Gospels regularly begins with the recitation of his genealogy. The child is not a spontaneous occurrence, but the current issue of many generations past. This genealogy and the broader network of relationships in which Christ, the Word, is enmeshed provide an alternative source of stability—alternative, that is, to the stability that would come from sublime, eternal fixity. This child—this Word—is, like all our words, rooted in a lineage and history. Those who talk to inform—and who would sublime the logic of language—would worry that if we allow our words to take their sense from the earth, they might come to mean anything and so nothing; such people think intelligibility cannot be truly supported apart from eternal fixity of meaning. But the sense of human rootedness the Christ bears with him—not only his genealogy, but his life in Nazareth with a household life and ordinary work—these human entanglements do not make it impossible for us to understand him. Rather, by giving him flesh, these contexts give life and sense to the Word.

Touch is Irigaray's most vibrant metaphor for talking about Christ's relation to the world. His touch is not violent nor from a great distance. It is not destructive of nor indifferent to mortal life. His miracles often work by his touching someone—the eyes of a blind man, for example—and at least once by his being touched by someone, the woman who reached out to his garment. He knew love also through being touched—one thinks of the woman anointing him with perfume, rubbing his skin with her hair. His body is even now how he gives himself and his love to the world eucharistically.

"Even his words," Irigaray writes, "aim to touch rather than to prove or convince. His teaching is almost always contradictory, and converts or heals by touching."[21] But what does it mean for a word to touch? If we distract ourselves with what Irigaray calls the *letter*, we may hear without understanding, as many of Christ's observers did. The letter in all its explicitness is yet too cryptic, and it remains outside the body; it is never made flesh. When we attend to the letter only, we may think we have no stake in the words; we may take them to be abstract and not see how we are implicated in them, or we may take them to be so straightforward as to require no attention. A word that touches affects one deeply, in time and over time; it is a *close* word, one pondered in one's heart. It grows over and in time, and it does not always try to inform with perfect clarity or guarantee its proper reception and interpretation. A word that touches is a word that one has taken in and nurtured; thus it is a word that has been offered as invitation or as balm. The word that touches lives in and through me as Christ lived in and through Mary before being sent forth into his own life. A word touches because it is not wholly familiar nor wholly strange. A word touches only out of a sense of intimacy or a life shared.

The incarnation of Christ, the Word, is the story of a new kind of divine advent: a divine being who comes not with violence that obliterates the mortal, a divine being who comes as an intimate rather than a distant otherworldly ruler, a divine being who comes not to take up and then abandon bodies to madness and endless passion. Christ does not manifest a perfection that is ultimately alien to men and women nor is he known only through writing, as a dead letter. Instead, he is made flesh. He is close to himself and close to others from and as his living body. And, as Irigaray writes, his living body can be affected by pathos.[22] The Logos suffers; the divine Logos is not sublime. So why do we think our language must aim at something better or more pure? Perhaps because we have done so little to try to understand what a desublimed Logos might look like. Our imagination for his vibrant appearance has withered as we have mourned his death and absence.

Christ, the God-man, does not live in "triumphant self-sufficiency." Instead he lives with others: "Always he is in society, in company, loved, helped. Living in a society of living people, from which he does not emerge as a solitary man. Sharing needs and desires with mortals."[23] Christ lives a life in time in history, and he knows bodily needs and limits. He, very God, also knows human emotions and experiences. He knows friendship and betrayal, confusion and clarity, desire and satisfaction. He is affected. And his sense of himself and any sense he has of the meaning of his life was given him by others. The meanings of the very Word of God are left to the care of those who surround him and know him, as well as those who cast him aside.

I said above that the vitality of words is close to the heart of our anxiety about them. Our words are our issue, but they also have lives of their own. They can wander off the paths we send them on. They can go places we had not imagined. They can fall flat. They can show up in unexpected places, in unforeseen guises, startling us or at least drawing our notice again. They live alongside us, with us; we live through them. But they can never belong exclusively to us; they are always hyperbolic. Father and mother are faithful to their son, the Word, who speaks in his voice. Neither controls the meaning nor the life of their issue. They both live in faithfulness to what lives outside the sovereignty of each. Our words likewise cannot live without us; they can have no meaning apart from our lives lived in time and history. But also they do live without us; they wander off, they refuse to stay in place, they return to us. They are prodigal. As we parent words in ourselves and in others, again and again, we make our way in risk and joy, sorrow and vitality, darkness and light.

What do we want to accomplish when we speak with one another? When we talk, we surrender our words, and in our more honest moments we admit that we cannot control how they are understood. Words are essentially receptive. To understand why we speak, then, is not to understand the mechanism by which meaning is transmitted. Rather it is to understand that our words are made into something as a joint venture between listener and speaker. Words are not tools for fully revealing myself to another. They do not allow me to make my mind perfectly and transparently known. Meaning-giving is joint, and that plurivocity is a source of life. The limits on my ability entirely to control how I am understood draw me into life with others. Communication entails an implicit trust; I surrender my words to my interlocutors or readers in the hope that they—in concert with me—will make something fruitful of my offering. Communication is communion.

Do we speak to inform? Or do we speak out of a sense of shared intimacy, a form of communion? Irigaray asks: what if Nietzsche heard a voice not his own? She imagines a feminine figure who might appear to him as other by stressing her freedom in the face of an opposing will. Such a figure of difference might cause—or allow—him finally to lose himself. "She is your labyrinth, you are hers. A path from you to yourself is lost in her, and from her to herself is lost in you."[24] This loss of a pathway is a blessed release. "Unless difference is affirmed, the inclusion of you in her, and her in you, spins off into a labyrinthine mourning for desire or for will inside you both (vous) and between you both."[25] Irigaray articulates the same question in a different key: did God hear Mary's voice (or merely an echo of his own voice)? Without her (uncoerced) yes, the nativity would have been the birth only of the same. Irigaray invites us to imagine that Mary speaks in her own voice, and, in speaking, she appears in her irreducibility. Her response is a real response, fully her own and fully faithful to what she knew of life. Her yes—*her* yes—introduces difference into the incarnation, and so makes all the difference, interrupting the endless loop (a kind of eternal recurrence) from Father to Son, same to same, always circling back to eternity and the selfsame will of the Father. The Father desires Mary in her irreducible difference. "Any detour is valuable if it can hide this revelation: the divine wishes to dwell in the flesh. The most glaring part of the rejection of this advent is—to lay a ban upon the flesh itself. To set Christ up as an idol of incarnation?"[26] The divine wishes to dwell in the flesh, desires the body, desires a body. This desire, this faithfulness to the flesh, issues forth in a living Word—and a salvation that is not indifferent to life in the flesh. A living word: given life by the mutual obsession of body and spirit.

Why does the Father speak? Who dares say? The constellation of desire, word, and incarnate life Irigaray proposes is provocative. Christ, the very Word of God, was born in Nazareth of his mother Mary. He walked the earth, touched and was touched, knew joy and perplexity in his relationships with others. His is not a life valorizing what is immutable, impregnable, and distant. Christ gives us access to eternity, to be sure, but it is an eternity intimate with flesh and time. It invites us to imagine a meaning not mortgaged to a heavenly beyond: a divine being who desires real intimacy with creation, a form of speaking that delivers us into a life with others, and a connection with the divine—and with others—that is fruitful and full of grace. Irigaray's portrait of Mary, her divine partner, and her infant Word, reminds us that Word comes to life in the context of intimacy and desire. We turn now to Augustine's own portrait of the inner teacher. It is more sparingly drawn, but no less rich in possibility.

CHAPTER SIX

CHRIST'S LIFE

If it is true that the inner teacher is not simply a power of informing, what then does the inner teacher *do*? What is his activity? How might we understand his role or purpose? In this chapter I examine two Augustinian portraits of Christ, the inner teacher. The first is Augustine's explicit description of the inner teacher toward the end of *De magistro*, where Augustine identifies him as Christ, the teacher of all men. The second portrait can be found in Augustine's retelling of the mystical vision at Ostia, where Augustine and his mother learn under the tutelage of that teacher. The inner teacher who emerges through these portraits is no informer of minds but rather one who draws interlocutors into his life. The presence of the inner teacher reminds Augustine, Adeodatus, and Monica that they do not make sense of words from a radically private place, distant from other creatures. Nor does meaning come from a divine father who is indifferent to time-bound life. Instead, through conversation both elevated and mundane, the inner teacher summons Augustine and his interlocutors into an intimate, shared space of meaning, rooted in the life they share with each other and with him.

Apart from a brief mention toward the beginning of *De magistro*, Christ, the teacher, does not appear until the closing pages of the dialogue. Why does his presence bookend the conversation? Why does Augustine return to him only as he winds down the dialogue? Driven by Augustine's provisional insistence that we speak only to inform, much of the first half of the dialogue examines how words function as signs to inform others. The conclusions of the first half of the dialogue are that (1) we talk to inform and (2) nothing can be taught—no one can be informed—without signs. These conclusions do not rest on any presuppositions about the working of the inner teacher, who remains unmentioned throughout these discussions. Perhaps Augustine does not associate Christ, the teacher, with these conclusions because they will shortly be overturned.

The figure of the inner teacher reappears as Augustine finds his way back to his opening theme of desire. The dialogue began with a question about desire: what do we want (*uelle*) to accomplish when we speak together? Augustine and Adeodatus spend the first part of the dialogue examining how the desire to inform might be satisfied. They neglect to acknowledge the full scope of desires motivating human speaking, but the neglect looks to be intentional, at least on Augustine's part, because it leads to the collapse of those conclusions that ought not and cannot stand. Questioning all that they have established so far, Augustine encourages his son to consider the suggestion—so different from how they began—that nothing is taught with signs. In this way, Augustine obliquely recalls his initial theme of desire, but he shifts the focus of their conversation from the desire to inform to the desire to understand. Augustine explicitly connects the desire to understand with the inner teacher, who plays a central role in the closing pages. Put simply, the fuller picture of human desire and the fuller portrait of the inner teacher emerge together.

If we speak with one another not just to inform but also to understand, we do not need clarity and perfection of word use. Instead we need habits of attention—perhaps even a disposition to faithfulness, though not necessarily of a religious sort. Returning to the question whether someone could be taught anything without signs, Augustine invites Adeodatus to imagine a bird catcher walking down the road, carrying all the tools of his trade (twigs, birdlime, etc.), without putting them to their proper use (*mag.* 10.32). Augustine adds to the scene a second person, a man ignorant of the art of bird snaring. This man, seeing the outfitted bird catcher, desires to know how and to what purpose the bird catcher uses his equipment. He need not wonder long. The bird catcher notices the curiosity of the other man. Seeing a bird, he puts his equipment to its proper use, catching and subduing the bird, under the attentive gaze of the second man. In such a case, concludes Augustine, has not the bird catcher taught the on-looker what he desired to understand, without the use of any sign what-soever? The bird catcher has informed someone not by means of pointing and signs but by showing the thing itself (i.e., bird snaring) to a curious and attentive observer.

Adeodatus is unconvinced. He wonders aloud whether they still face the same problems of misapprehension involved in ostensive definitions of walking, that is, that it is difficult to show *walking* unambiguously, with-out showing, say, *hurrying* or *talking* or *changing location*. How can the bird catcher show bird snaring as distinguished from wren snaring or animal-catching-with-a-net? He also voices his doubt that the whole art of bird snaring could be taught so quickly. In reply, Augustine stipulates an ob-server so quick at understanding that he learns the art of bird snaring from the one display. Clever Adeodatus, seeing that such a move might rescue them from their earlier difficulties, likewise stipulates a man who might un-derstand exactly what *walking* is from just one short display. Augustine wel-comes the suggestion, noting that thousands of things can be demonstrated without signs. Performances in theaters, the sun, the moon, the stars, and all the earth are revealed to us simply as we look at them (*mag.* 10.32).

Yet the quality of the looking matters. We can look without seeing. Augustine suggests we will not gain understanding without desire and at-tention. The man learns the art of bird snaring because, desiring to know, he gives his attention to the activity of the bird catcher. Well-focused at-tention can reveal the very things we want to know, that is, not just words and other signs, but the realities toward which they point. My gaze can take the form of a question, and my interlocutor, be it an idling bird catcher or even the creator of the world, can answer my query without using any sign at all.[1]

After remarking that thousands of things can be demonstrated without signs, Augustine pushes forward into the more radical claim that nothing is demonstrated or revealed by its sign. He explains, "If a sign is mentioned to me, and I am caught unaware of what it signifies, it cannot inform me. But if I already know [the thing it signifies], what has the sign informed me of?"[2] If I do not already know what a word signifies, it reveals nothing to me when I hear it. If someone utters a word unfamiliar to me (especially a word out of context), I will not understand what it signifies.

Augustine's example from this category is the word *sarabarae* from the story of the fiery furnace in the book of Daniel (*mag.* 10.33). When Augustine first read the passage, the word (a Latinized form of an Aramaic term) meant nothing to him. If he had been told that *sarabarae* are a kind of head covering, the words *head* and *covering* would not have informed Augustine of their own meanings. He already knew those meanings. And he learned what *head* and *covering* mean not because they were called by those sounds, but because he had seen those things for himself. All unfamiliar words are initially just sounds to me; a word becomes a sign for me only when I recognize the thing signified: "a sign is learned from a known thing, more than a thing is learned from the mention of a sign."[3] I may figure out the meaning of a word like *head* because someone points at heads repeatedly while saying the word, but the pointing (itself a sign) does not give me knowledge of the head (which I had before I knew the sign) nor of the sign. The pointing encourages me to look, but it cannot make me see and understand. The seeing and understanding are motivated (or not) by my desire. Therefore, Augustine concludes, we are not taught by the signs we call words: "For . . . we learn the power of a word—its meaning, hidden in the sound—from the known reality, which is signified, not from grasping that reality through signification."[4] We learn by looking, by seeing a thing and connecting it with a sound; the words themselves and even the pointing do not teach us. Augustine summarizes: "When I learned the reality itself, I did not trust another's words, but my own eyes—though I may have trusted those words to direct my attention and seeking. Thus, by looking, I came to understanding."[5] Words can summon and direct our attention, but they cannot inform us of anything.

If what we want is understanding, our attention should not rest only in words themselves. Well-handled words are not a sufficient condition for understanding. Augustine, accomplished rhetorician, surely knows this from experience. He therefore reminds his son to be attentive to the reality toward which words point. As signs, words draw attention to things, to experience, to reality, and—he will explain several pages later—to the inner teacher. Augustine writes,

> The most credit I would give to words is this: they summon us to seek and know a thing, but they do not make a thing known. The

one who teaches me presents to my eyes or to any bodily sense or to my mind, those things I want to know. From words, we learn nothing but words—just their sound and noise. For since things that are not signs cannot be words, when I have heard a word, I don't even know whether it is a word, until I know what it signifies.[6]

Augustine's point, of course, is not that words and other signs do not matter. Words serve the important purpose of summoning our attention to the realities we desire to know.

Augustine deliberately oversimplifies here. I am confident the simplification is deliberate, because he complicates the picture just a few pages later. The simple picture Augustine describes may seem straightforward enough when it comes to visible objects. Consider an example. I, beginning my study of the German language at the age of thirteen, learned what a *Geschirrspülmaschine* was by being given other, simpler words that pointed me toward the image in my memory of a dishwasher. But the simple picture of signification breaks down if I try to teach someone the name of something that does not readily present itself to the eye of the body or of the mind. While I am fairly confident my two-year-old and I mean the same thing when we say the word *breakfast* (or *BREFF-ixt*, as he pronounces it), I am less confident he and I mean the same thing when we say *I love you*. Maybe I do not even know that my husband and I mean the same thing when we utter those words to each other. How do I connect the word *love* with some reality—love—with which I am already familiar? What is that reality, and how can I recognize it? Augustine's simple picture also breaks down when words naming physical objects are used figuratively. I can teach my toddler what an apple is by pointing at the contents of our fruit bowl. But that ostensive definition does not convey much. He will come to learn, in time, that talking about an apple in a Christian theological context is quite different from talking about an apple-cheeked youth, while both are different from the fruit we eat or the technology company. Love, apples, and many other realities, both visible and invisible, complicate Augustine's tidy picture. We simply can never be *certain* we have communicated those realities and understood one another without ambiguity. And yet most of us, most of the time, are not tormented by the ambiguities of language. We get along fine. Augustine and Adeodatus seem to get along fine too.

Augustine skirts similar difficulties of ambiguity as he plays out the *sarabarae* example (*mag.* 11.37). He says we know from reading Scripture that the three young men who wore *sarabarae* sang, earned praise from their persecutors, and overcame those persecutors by their faith and piety. Those of us who live at a temporal distance from those events may be tempted to say that we learned those truths through words, but Augustine insists that we could not know the meanings of the words apart from knowledge of the things. It is worth noting Augustine does not draw attention to the tremendously interesting difficulty of learning what faith and piety are, nor to the lack of certainty we might have about whether we mean the same thing by those terms as others do.[7] The words *faith* and *piety*, like the word *love*, certainly raise problems of ambiguity and agreement. Yet Augustine passes all these difficulties by without comment. He is not naïve about the possibilities of misapprehension and miscommunication—he mentions them explicitly later in the dialogue. Such possibilities exist, making themselves more or less troublesome. What I take from the omission here is that Augustine does not take the messiness of human discourse as a problem to be solved. Our biggest problem with words and speaking, he hints, is not misunderstanding and misapprehension but failure of attention.

Throughout this book, I have criticized problematic readings of the inner teacher of *De magistro*. I wish now, for the sake of tidiness, that I could offer my own Augustinian account of the function of the inner teacher. I cannot. The inner teacher is a partner in meaning giving, but he cannot be instrumentalized. As Augustine describes him, the inner teacher invites us to love and be loved, to understand and be understood. He works in and through our shared, embodied, temporal lives and limitations. The inner teacher comes to us through the words of those with whom we speak and the life we share. This is fitting, since that teacher is, according to Christian tradition, the one through whom all things were made.

The words others speak summon our attention to the inner voice of truth, the wisdom of God (*mag.* 11.38). The image, as Augustine gives it, resists theorizing. Father tells son,

> Concerning all those things we understand [*intellegimus*], we do
> not turn to a speaker making noise outside, but within, to the truth

which keeps vigil over the mind—though words may have summoned [*admoniti*] us to turn to that truth. Christ, who is said to
live in the inner man, is the one to whom we turn there, the one
who teaches us. He is the immutable power of God and everlasting
wisdom. Every reasoning spirit turns to him, but what is revealed is
only as much as one can grasp, according to one's own disposition,
whether evil or good. If sometimes one is deceived, it is not the fault
of the truth consulted, just as the light outside is not to blame when
the eyes of the body are deceived. And we acknowledge we turn to
this light when it comes to visible things, so that it might make them
clear to us, to the extent we can make them out.[8]

The inner teacher does not facilitate the filling of minds. Rather, through
the words of others, he summons us. When we understand, we do not learn
from words or from the speaker who voices them. We learn by listening to
the inner truth who keeps vigil over our minds. We reason by listening to
the changeless power of God and his wisdom. The inner teacher does not
simply affirm or correct my hunches and beliefs. Instead truth watches over
us, like a mother over a newborn.

Yet it is difficult to listen well to that wisdom. If this teacher speaks to
our minds in order that we might understand truth, we may wonder why
Augustine is so concerned about our *disposition* toward the inner teacher.
He writes that the inner teacher responds according to each person's evil
or good disposition or sentiment (*uoluntatem*; *mag.* 11.38). I grasp as much
as is given to me according to my own *uoluntas*. Sometimes I refuse to listen to that wisdom. But Augustine's metaphor is difficult to understand.
How could I *not* learn from the inner teacher who has a direct line into my
mind? Would not his informing of my mind be inescapable? If this teacher
is my direct line to truth, what might make me deaf to that? How could
my bad disposition or will make it difficult for my mind's ear to hear truth?
What could motivate me to resist the voice of the inner teacher, who wants
to speak truth to me?

Augustine's emphasis on *uoluntas* at this point recalls again his opening
question about desire (*uelle*). What do we want when we speak with one
another? As he begins to expand his artificially restricted account of language, he hints too at a dilation of desire. Do we want to inform? Do we

want to be informed? Do we want only to be understood? Or do we want wisdom? The inner teacher speaks, but I do not always hear. He and I can become estranged or alienated. Then I cannot make sense of his voice, cannot make it fit with what I know of the world. It falls silent for me. Augustine asks his son and us, his readers, whether we desire to continue listening to that teacher and seeking Christ's life, in and through our life with others.

Cultivating attentiveness to the voice of the inner teacher turns out to be no solitary matter. Our conversations can help us become more attentive to it. Augustine tells Adeodatus, "If I were to ask you whether it is true that nothing can be taught by words—the very thing we are discussing—at first the question might seem absurd, if you were not able to grasp the matter as a whole. In that case, I would need to ask you questions to nurture your capacities [*uires*] for paying attention to that teacher within."[9] In *De magistro*, Augustine does not inform Adeodatus, but, through their conversation, he does help his son to understand something. That understanding comes through their mutual attentiveness to each other, to their experience, and to the wisdom of God speaking within each of them.

Augustine challenges the temptation to focus myopically on words and their power. Words cannot fix meanings in the minds of others. What they can do is help us attend to the voice of the inner teacher. This fact explains why Augustine is unperturbed in *De magistro* by ambiguities of word use, as when words do not fully reflect the thoughts of the speaker (*mag.* 13.42), or when words have different meanings to different groups of people (*mag.* 13.43), or when someone mishears a word spoken correctly (*mag.* 13.44). None of these occasional problems need trouble him, for perfection of word use is not the point. Perfection only matters when I am deluded enough to think that another's understanding depends on it.

Ambiguities of reference are not the heart of our need. The inner teacher teaches us something much more profound: how to know and love. In the case of the word *sarabarae*, Augustine proposed that his pre-existing knowledge of a thing is the basis for his recognition of a particular word as a sign for that thing. Now he presents his son with a substantially more difficult case: the meaning of the words *in heaven* (*mag.* 14.46). Augustine hopes aloud he and his son might not merely believe (*crederemus*) but understand (*intellegere*) the scriptural declaration that no one on earth can be rightly called our teacher: "For now, as I have reminded you, we should not give words more credit than is due. Therefore, we should not merely believe but begin to understand how truly it has been written, by divine authority, that we should call no one on earth our teacher. The one teacher of all is in heaven."[10] This teacher will teach us the meaning of the words *in heaven*.

Learning the meaning of the words *in heaven* and using those words intelligibly with others is much more difficult than mastering terms for items of clothing, to say the least. Do the words *in heaven* name a reality with which I am already familiar? For most of us, the answer is surely no. Nonetheless, we use those words. Given the thinness of scholarly attention to these words, we might be tempted to think Augustine's choice of the words *in heaven* was nearly arbitrary—that he could just as easily have said that the inner teacher teaches us what *apple* or *quarterback* means. Granting the difficulties of ostension and the possibilities of misapprehension, I have some grasp on the meanings of those terms (more so for apples, less so for quarterbacks). But it is hard to imagine what it would mean to have a similar grasp on the meaning of the words *in heaven*. Augustine tells Adeodatus they will be taught (*docebit*) what *in heaven* means, by the inner teacher. The use of the future tense signals that this meaning is not already known to them, even though they already use those words. Perhaps they have a working sense of what those words mean, but they hope they will grow into a deeper sense of that meaning.

The meaning of the words *in heaven* is not a bit of information, a preformed meaning they wait to receive from the master informer. The relevant Latin sentence packs a lot into one syntactical unit, implying that the meaning of these two words is bound up with something much deeper than preventing confusion and misunderstanding. The sentence begins with the promise that the teacher within will teach them what *in heaven* means and ends with the desire to live the blessed life through loving and knowing that teacher. Augustine explains,

What *in heaven* means, he himself will teach us—he who through external human signs turns our attention inward to him so that we, turned, might be taught. Loving and knowing him make up the blessed life, which all claim to desire, but few know the delight of having found.[11]

The inner teacher will teach us the meaning of the words *in heaven.* We will learn that meaning from him, the one whom to love and to know (*diligere ac nosse*) is the blessed life. As we know and love him, he acquaints us with the reality of the life most blessed (*mag.* 14.46). It is important to emphasize that Augustine does not say that our words are simply an occasion or opening for Christ to do the real work of informing minds.[12] The verbal signs of those with whom we speak do matter. They are significant. As they signify *rei*, they point us toward the inner teacher. Outward signs turn us toward him and to the life he offers us.

During Augustine's description of the limits of words and the figure of the inner teacher, Adeodatus is curiously silent, as he had been for more than a dozen pages. But his remarks at the end of the dialogue show that he has been paying careful attention, reflecting on the realities toward which his father gestures. Adeodatus summarizes the highlights: words can do nothing more than summon us to learning, words cannot reveal the thoughts of those who speak them, and Christ teaches whether true things are said. He concludes, "With his help, I will love him more ardently the more I progress in learning."[13] Adeodatus's cogent and elegant summary is hardly the end of the story. He is a brilliant young man, beginning his education, as well as a newly baptized Christian, beginning to know the love of Christ. Father's and son's conclusions are not the end of the conversation nor the end of their learning what heaven is. Their conclusions are not the end of meaning, but its promise.

Augustine makes good on his assurance to Adeodatus that their conversation is not devoid of significance. By suggesting that their conversation about words has something to do with living the blessed life, Augustine reminds his son and his readers of the transformative possibilities within conversation with others, both divine and human. Much as I might try to use language to contract my world down to manageable size, to try to get a fix on meaning, to try to articulate my desires without acknowledgment of the forces, personalities, and gifts that give shape to those desires—in a word, much as I try to use language to inform—my speaking belies those attempts. Speaking draws me into a life with others, where many author and give shape to that life. As I speak with others, becoming more at ease with the limits of my language, I do not parse the boundaries of meaning more carefully. Rather I learn to love and hear the voice of God. Encountering the limits of my ability to use words to inform transforms not just my approach to language but my understanding of the truly happy life. If Augustine's initial remarks in *De magistro* contract the possibilities of words, he ultimately shows how this contraction is part of being delivered into a life most blessed.

Confessiones 9 contains mention of two important and related conversations: the exchange of *De magistro* (briefly noted) and the conversation between Augustine and his mother at Ostia (narrated in full). The latter took place less than two years before the former, and they are separated by mere pages in the text of the *Confessiones*. From a retrospective point of view, the parallels between the two conversations are striking. Both conversations occur not long before the death of one of the participants. Both express the interlocutors' longing to know the reality of heaven. In both, familial conversation provides the context for an encounter with divine wisdom. Most significantly, both contain portraits of the inner teacher who speaks through the intimacy of a shared life.

The conversation at Ostia was liminal. Ostia was an ancient Roman port city whose name derives from *os*, the Latin word for mouth. Augustine and his entourage rest there in preparation for their journey back to North Africa. Augustine's mother Monica, however, will not return home with the others. She will soon undertake an even more significant journey, to the very gates of heaven. Before that departure, however, mother and son enjoy conversation about the life of the blessed souls in heaven. Their conversation is often termed a vision—and rightly so. What mother and son receive does not have its source solely in their own minds and hearts. Yet the wisdom they receive does not arrive from out of the blue, like Zeus's bolt of lightning. Augustine's staging of the scene as a shared conversation suggests that the intimacy between the two informs the encounter with divine wisdom. The wisdom of God is revealed in a shared space of meaning.

Augustine and his mother stand together, he tells us in his *Confessiones*, leaning out of a window overlooking a garden (*conf.* 9.10.23). The garden stands as a metaphor for an interior place, but the image suggests an expansive sense of interiority. It is enclosed but is also a meeting place. It is protected from the outside world, but open to the heavens. This garden at Ostia is at the center of the house and at the center of the hearts of mother and son, who stand there together and apart.[14] In this garden, mother and son move toward an intimacy that becomes a shared experience of self-transcendence. Here interiority is shared, a place where mother and son stand together.

Monica and Augustine speak together very intimately about eternity and the eternal life of the saints (*conf.* 9.10.23).[15] As they speak, the pleasures of the body seem to pale by comparison with that life, and mother and son long to know Being itself: "raising ourselves in more ardent affection toward *That Which Is*, we traveled, step by step, past all bodily creatures and heaven itself, whence sun and moon and stars shine down on the earth."[16] Through inward thought, conversation, and wondering about the works of God (*interius cogitando et loquendo et mirando opera tua; conf.* 9.10.24), Augustine and Monica transcend even their own minds and touch that realm where Israel is pastured with the food of truth. As they talk and pant for that wisdom, they touch it by a leap of their hearts (*conf.* 9.10.24).[17] Then, with a sigh, they return to the noise of their speech, where words begin and end (*conf.* 9.10.24).

Augustine calls the object of his and Monica's contemplation the wisdom of God (*conf.* 9.10.24)—the same title he gives to the inner teacher in *De magistro* (*mag.* 11.38). While they encounter this wisdom in circumstances somewhat removed from ordinary life, their glimpse of heaven is no repudiation of incarnate human life. The wisdom they touch is the very wisdom that created all things—including the life they share. Augustine describes that life in its perfected form in heaven: "Life there is the wisdom through whom all these things are made, both those that were and those that will be. Wisdom herself is not made, but is as she has been and as she always will be."[18] That divine wisdom is not identical with the life mother and son were living, but it is the source and the hope of their life. It is the wisdom that created Augustine and gave him new life in baptism, that life he had recently come to share with his mother.

In crafting his *Confessiones*, Augustine places his memory of the Ostia conversation between two bookends: a remembrance of his mother's life and a remembrance of the events surrounding her death. By means of this framing, Augustine signals that the conversation is situated within the context and history of the lives they lead together. That history includes Monica's peaceable speech, which Augustine says she learned from her "*intimate teacher*, Christ, in the school of her heart."[19] The conversation at Ostia is tethered to their lives, and the voice of the inner teacher is heard in the midst of those who speak with one another within the bonds of charity and a life shared. Monica and Augustine, like Augustine and Adeodatus, hear the wisdom of God speaking within their conversation with one another. The ecstasy and its insight are given shape by the inexhaustible richness of their life, which is not only their own but hidden in Christ.

Mother and son share this experience without losing either themselves or each other. They are not deaf to each other, nor are they obliterated by being subsumed into the God whom they seek. Augustine stands in physical proximity to his mother and in communion with her, even as he knows intimacy with divine wisdom. The pattern of ascent is pursued by each soul, and the object of their experience is the same. Even the words they speak are recorded by Augustine as joint, not distinguished according to person. Augustine's narration of the event in the first person plural highlights the fact that "the common context in which they stand does not swallow them up."[20] Their conversation, their speaking and hearing, sustains the community between the two of them as they touch the transcendent wisdom of God.

The wisdom they encounter is not fully captured by signs, though signs can and do point them toward it. Augustine describes their dialogue as conversation, saying they speak with one another (*loquimur*), even though their speaking together becomes inaudible at the highest point of the vision. They encounter wisdom in a form beyond audible words, and they agree human words will be superfluous in heaven. Nevertheless, in the aftermath of the vision, they still find they have words to share. Mother and son return to audible conversation to reflect on what they have touched with their hearts. In a lyrical denouement, they imagine all creatures and every sound falling silent. In heaven, they say to each other, there is no more speaking together. There the faithful hear the Word of God not through tongues or voices or any kind of sign, but simply as himself. What is signified in mortal life will be encountered, unmediated, then. Heaven is nothing else, mother and son agree, than listening to this wisdom in an unmediated way. Eternal life is an act of perfect attention.

The conversation at Ostia is not a matter of teaching or informing. Monica and Augustine bask in truth, spurring each other on to greater love of that life—Christ's life—that binds them together. Though Augustine crafts his retelling of the vision carefully, he admits that part or all of the conversation may not have taken place in precisely the words he has set down (*conf.* 9.10.26).[21] The words themselves are not the point. Augustine takes this distance from his words not to signal a faulty memory but to acknowledge the difficulty of speaking about an encounter with God. The language that occurs to him and to Monica is a figurative and incarnate one, full of images, connoting abundance and intimacy, both with God and with each other. Such language does not allow them to get a fix on meaning, but gestures toward the overabundance of their experience.[22] Mother and son have heard the wisdom of God, speaking to them of heaven, and they still find they have words at heart to share with one another—figurative ways of speaking that proliferate meanings within the space between them. If the *regio dissimilitudinis* of *Confessiones* 7 is a desert, stripped bare of all that might mislead or confuse, Augustine and Monica's conversation is a lush garden, endlessly fruitful. It is there they learn the meaning of *in heaven*, as they continue to help each other find their way into that life.

Augustine's two portraits of the inner teacher suggest an expansive sense of interiority, where interiority is not characterized by privacy but by intimacy. Christ is the inner teacher because he is intimate to us—more intimate than we are to ourselves, Augustine tells us (*conf.* 3.6.11). Christ is also intimate to those with whom we speak. This intimacy is rooted in love. He loves us, and he desires love from us. Augustine helps us see how much that love is bound up with a quality of attention. Christ teaches us not how to inform the minds of others, but how to be more attentive to the possibilities of meaning. He does this by summoning our attention both to himself and to those with whom we speak. These forms of attention may turn out to be the same thing.

The inner teacher helps us notice the meanings emerging within the life we share with others. The words of others, Augustine writes, summon us to turn to the truth who keeps vigil over our minds. That truth, that teacher, illuminates the life we share with others. He sustains an intimate space of meaning that forms the ground of our most profound forms of intelligibility. For Augustine, a line of Virgil evokes a lost mother. A Punic word recalls a moment of mutual confusion. A recent conversion enlivens a desire to understand the most blessed life of the saints. Words are heavy with possibilities, given form by the lives of those who speak them. Augustine's conversations remind us that we are able to speak most meaningfully with each other inasmuch as we learn to love and attend to the life we share in Christ.[23] That life is where the inner teacher speaks.[24] It is the matrix from which meaning is born.

The most important teaching of the inner teacher is his invitation into the blessed life. The beata vita is the life of Christ, and it is a life he desires to share with us, both on earth and in heaven. As we speak together, our best hope is that we might help birth each other into the life most blessed, a life of knowing and loving Christ through attentiveness to him and to those he loves. Augustine's images of birth and life suggest an interiority that is intimate but not private—an interiority woven together with the lives of others. Christ, as inner teacher, summons us not to some inner citadel of meaning, but to something more like a womb, a source of nourishment and life. To love the inner teacher is to be invited into a life incarnate, a life with others in him, a life more abundant than I could conceive alone.

CHAPTER SEVEN

WORDS, AFTERWARD

De magistro opens with Augustine's question to Adeodatus: "What do we want to accomplish when we speak with one another?" Given the untimely and unexpected death of the young man, we might recast Augustine's question in a way that takes account of that loss: "What do we want when we speak with those we will lose?" Augustine and Monica's conversation about heaven took place in the penumbra of Monica's death. Augustine and Adeodatus's discussion had no such context, at least not wittingly. Yet their conversation is an important part of how Augustine remembers the boy after his death. In *Confessiones* 9, he praises his son's brilliance and refers to the dialogue as *our book* (*liber noster*). Their conversation about the meaning of the words *in heaven* may have come back to Augustine, grieving father, as unexpected consolation.

When Augustine's partner of fifteen years was sent away, the boy Adeodatus stayed with his father. We do not know what prompted this arrangement, though we might guess it relieved economic burdens on the boy's mother and allowed Adeodatus an education overseen by his successful and highly educated father.[1] Whatever the reasons for the living situation, the boy was Augustine's last connection to the woman to whom he had given his heart. The boy's flesh was made of hers. His life was buoyed by promise. His death, at about seventeen years of age, was unexpected, probably the result of a sudden illness. We do not know whether Augustine was able to inform the boy's mother.[2] We do know that no one, apart from her, could understand how much this loss left Augustine bereft.

Augustine says little about his grief over his son, either in the *Confessiones* or elsewhere. Despite his lyrical descriptions of his grief over his friend, Augustine is silent about the tremendous pain the death of his son surely brought. When Augustine recalls Adeodatus's death, he gives his reader no descriptions of heartsick wandering through the city, no overwrought laments and regrets. Ever the subtle shaper of his story, Augustine recalls his son by accenting not heart-shattering loss, but hope. As a psychological fact, we can be sure the pain of his loss was acute. But Augustine memorializes his son not with an account of his own pain but with attention to the person his son was. That is, of course, the only memorial worthy of the name.

It is difficult to speak about what is closest to one's heart. Augustine's recollection of the boy in *Confessiones* 9 is accordingly brief. In contrast to his lengthy remembrance of Monica, Augustine's tribute to Adeodatus takes up only half a page (*conf.* 9.6.14). He writes there that the brilliance of young Adeodatus filled him with awe. Even at the age of fifteen, "his innate talent was superior to many eminent and learned men."[3] The intellectual gifts of Adeodatus shine especially brightly in *De magistro*. Augustine notes that all the thoughts attributed to Adeodatus in the dialogue were really his.[4] He prays, "His talent astonished me, for who but you could be the artificer of such miracles?"[5] His remembrance is a cause for wonder and gratitude in Augustine, who praises God for the gifts of his son (*conf.* 9.6.14).

Augustine's son is beautiful, a wonder. Yet his father, brilliant in his own right, takes no credit for the miracle the boy is. He identifies not himself but God as creator of this wonder. "I confess your gifts to you, O Lord, my God, creator of all things and very powerful in reforming our deformities. For I had no part in that boy except my fault."[6] The term *fault* (*delictum*) presumably refers to Augustine's unmarried sexual intimacy with his partner of more than a decade, though that fault was not the only way Augustine fell short as a father. Augustine claims the boy was born from Augustine in the flesh, from his father's sin (*ex me natum carnaliter de peccato meo*; *conf.* 9.6.14), and the boy suffered for it, growing up motherless in a family torn apart by Augustine's and Monica's ambitions. Yet, whatever imperfections may have existed in the father's love, the primary note in Augustine's recollection is not self-criticism nor guilt, but gratitude: Augustine prays twice in the passage *munera tua tibi confiteor*, "your gifts I confess to you" (*conf.* 9.6.14).

Augustine tells readers he remembers the boy without anxiety. Adeodatus is his safe one. He writes it was God alone who inspired him and the boy's mother to feed (*nutriebatur*) the boy on the truth (*disciplina*) of the Lord (*conf.* 9.6.14). Father and mother nurtured the child, bringing him under the tutelage of the Lord, before his mother was sent back to her North African home. Years later, Adeodatus joined his father and Alypius in baptism in Milan. Because of this participation in the life of grace, Augustine finds he has no fear for the boy. Augustine's remembrance of Adeodatus reveals, above all, that the son does not belong to the father alone. Augustine, imperfect father that he is, is not his son's sole source and creator. The boy's life is held in love, by his mother, by the community of believers and friends into which he has been baptized, and most of all by God. This assurance is a blessed release to Augustine. A note of forgiveness sounds here. Augustine has some fault. All parents do. But the boy is full of grace.

Augustine's remembrance here summarizes two sides of the coin of a child's independence from his parent. Side one: My child's growing independence from my will is a relief, promising freedom for my child and myself. My child is not what I make or create. He can set out in new directions without being shackled by my imperfections and mistakes as a parent. In time, he can respond not out of obedience only but out of his love. This independence turns out to be a surprising (but real) form of grace. Side two is the shadow side: My child's independence from my will, from my absolute sphere of control, often means I cannot fix, cannot guarantee, cannot protect. My actions only play, often ineffectually, at the edge of what matters most. This can cause pain beyond reckoning. I cannot protect the bodies I love, to say nothing of their hearts. Can grace be found there too?

De magistro was probably published around 390, and Adeodatus likely died within a year of the dialogue's publication.[7] Whatever the precise timing might have been, the dialogue winds up serving as a memorial to the boy. It keeps the memory of Adeodatus alive, for Augustine and for others. Augustine's comments in *Confessiones* 9 make clear the dialogue is not just a memorial to brilliance—Augustine's as a teacher and Adeodatus's as a student. Augustine does not memorialize Adeodatus for his cleverness in sussing out a theory of signification in response to his father's questioning. No such theory is needed. They are already in conversation, making meaning together in fits and starts, and the connection—the intimacy—is already there. Instead Augustine's memories frame *De magistro* as a memorial to the fullness of the person of Adeodatus, as he is held in love by his absent mother, his imperfect father, and his gracious God. *De magistro* memorializes Adeodatus not as a dead child, but as a child of love.

The book is a memorial to the love and the life shared between the two. To acknowledge that fact is not to turn our attention as readers away from the significance of the conversation; instead it makes us better readers of that significance. What might it mean for a father to ask a brilliant and beloved son (*mag.* 1.1), "What do we want to accomplish when we speak with one another?" And what kind of answers could Augustine take comfort in having found, in conversation with his son, after Adeodatus's death? I have no interest in inventing the inner lives of these men after the fact. But it is hard to imagine that one who had lost his son—and felt the deep bonds of their familial connection—would find any sense in the claim that Christ, the inner teacher, arrives to supplant the father-son bond, to make possible understanding beyond the bonds of a shared life, and to motivate speech apart from the realities of human life. It is hard to imagine why Augustine would find any consolation in the notion that Christ makes possible disinterested and disincarnate communication.

Just as Christ is not some instrument by which Augustine and Adeodatus can make language function well, neither is love. Augustine's insight in *De magistro* is not that loving people provides some kind of cognitive and communicative benefits, however true that may be. Love is not simply another effective instrument for getting on with language, one that facilitates good listening or patience in confusion. I take Augustine's point here to be more descriptive than prescriptive. We misunderstand language when we think it serves to make a connection between self and other. That is backward. Language only works inasmuch as the connection is there.[8] We already have what we need. Love undergirds meaning. Already. The love Augustine describes is no sentimental feeling of affection, but, as Eric Gregory puts it, "a form of arresting attention that knows the dangers present within love for others."[9] Augustine invites us to attend to the ways our lives form meaning, more or less, in ways well beyond our control.

Throughout this book, I have argued against disincarnate and superficial readings that tend to strip out the so-called philosophical content of

De magistro from its conversational and familial context. The fact of the death of Adeodatus only reinforces the implausibility of such readings. His death, unanticipated at the time of the conversation, highlights the defects of the disincarnate readings and cannot but shape how we encounter the text now. We read the dialogue superficially only if we have a superficial sense of the meanings of words—if we think that the act of understanding the words *in heaven* is equivalent to the act of understanding the words *lemon squeezy*, and if we think that the men discuss signification with all the indifference of two clever but heartless minds.

Augustine's framing of *De magistro* as a memorial to a beloved son reinforces my argument that the text is not an explanation of how words inform the minds of others. The two impulses are at cross-purposes. Talking to inform tries to scale down meaning to rule out heartbreak. It tries to speak beyond the possibilities of loss. Talking to inform offers the illusory promise of putting interlocutors in contact with eternal meanings, meanings that can never be damaged or lost by connection with mortal human life. Talking to inform tries to speak beyond other kinds of losses too, the more routine losses of speaking words that fall flat or fail to connect. When we talk to inform, we mistakenly hope perfected sign-use will guarantee intelligibility, and we seek out safety and impregnability in our language. Augustine refuses such temptations and pretenses. The father's heart breaks. How could it not?

Augustine's text, read in its familial context, delicately reminds us of the profound ways that words are bound up with loss. No intelligibility comes apart from intimacy. Yet intimacy opens us to the possibilities of suffering and loss. Augustine's poignant conversations with Monica and Adeodatus, artfully framed in the *Confessiones* by the facts of their deaths, suggest a connection between grief and the extraordinary experiences of understanding Augustine describes. These memories of loss are not mere window-dressing for the conversations they flank. Love is both the ground of understanding and the site of a darkness that cannot be comprehended. Augustine's conversations with his son and his mother take place near the boundary of life and death, and it is that position—that proximity to the reality of life's mortality—that helps them to see what they see. Through this juxtaposition of insight and loss, Augustine affirms the goodness and beauty of what can suffer and be lost. We do not succeed as speakers only insofar as we can offer words that operate beyond the possibilities of opacity or loss.[10] To meet that standard we would, finally, have to give up speaking. The reality of human parting instead compels Augustine and his loved ones to unfold the depth of what they share.

In Samuel Beckett's *Endgame*, the character Hamm describes his impatience with a man who came to beg for bread for his dying child. A bit of bread might revive the boy temporarily, Hamm scoffs, but revival would only postpone his eventual death. He tells the desperate father, "Use your head, can't you, use your head, you're on earth, there's no cure for that!"[11] The near-to-death conversational limit cases Augustine describes remind us that we are always speaking with those near to death, more or less. We are always speaking with those from whom we will be separated in time. Yet Augustine draws from this reality no deflationary moral about the limited value of words. Instead he reminds us that our intimacy with others brings meaning to birth. There is no cure for mortality. We need not seek one. We can speak out of fragility, loss, and brokenness, knowing the life we share with others will hold us.

Loss is at the very heart of words. The bishop Augustine, reflecting in *Confessiones* on his performance of grief following the death of his friend, develops a discomfiting analogy between created beauties (like his friend) and the syllables of words (*conf.* 4.11.17–4.12.18). We love to cling to created beauties, to their detriment and ours, as Augustine bitterly discovered. With words, our approach is typically different. When you listen to human speech, Augustine reminds his soul (and his reader), "You do not want the syllables to halt. Instead, you want them to fly past, allowing others to come, so that you can hear the whole."[12] In setting up an analogy between created beauties and syllables, Augustine's point is emphatically not that we should dial down our love for created beauties. Augustine does not say that the whole is more valuable than the parts. Augustine's insight here is more subtle. The full meaning of the part, he urges, is only revealed as it slip-slides out of the speaker's grip and comes to take its place in relation to every other part. The stress is on the meaningfulness of the part, be it the syllable or the life of an individual. The revelation of the whole, rightly apprehended, only sharpens our attention to the particular.[13] Loss can be a revelation, even though it cuts to the bone.

Like most grief, Augustine's is complicated. As he reflects on what he has lost, he confesses his failures of love. His grief is expressive of his love, but that love—for his partner, for his son, for his mother—was, he admits, imperfect. He reminds us that the life we live, even in its imperfection and frailty, teaches us as we love. In *De magistro*, when Augustine turns his son toward Christ, his inner teacher, he shows the love of Christ is a common life in which they are both held, father and son. That life allows them to live with the gaps, hesitations, and losses. Christ's life is not an abstract principle of intelligibility, but a love that brings forgiveness and peace, allowing even a broken relationship—which is to say, a perfectly ordinary one—to be communicative. Love does not dissolve difference. It does not burn off the apparent chaff of hesitations and false starts, the ways we can be lost to each other and the ways speaking can leave us feeling profoundly alienated from one another. Augustine promises no escape from all that. The heartbreak will be there, even as we are being drawn out into the bright light of the *beata vita*. This is love's labor. While it is hard and sometimes seems to deliver us into darkness, it is also the very ground of understanding. If we are tempted to set intimacy and intelligibility at odds, we have failed to pay attention to the lives we live with others. Augustine's memorialization of Adeodatus is neither romantic nor tragic. It is clear-eyed. Augustine shows love not abstracted from bodies and places, not protected from sorrow and distance. He confesses love that abides through hesitations and lost threads, love that forgives all. For Augustine, beatitude is not a form of perfection based on humanly impossible standards.

Our recurrent sense of the darkness of communication will often be tied to the fact of our birth, our imprint on the world, and with the ways we experience birth as an impediment to knowledge and clarity. For those of us who live our lives in time and flesh, understanding can never be guaranteed. When we speak, we are sometimes lost to each other. There are moments of confusion, isolation, and hesitation or, worse, moments of harm, betrayal, and willful misunderstanding. In the face of that pain, we may be tempted to imagine that perfect intelligibility goes hand in hand (or mind in mind) with disincarnation. Augustine knows well the temptation to build alienation into the conditions for intelligibility. We think we speak in an illuminating way insofar as we speak clearly, impersonally, in exacting prose, free from dramatic and mundane entanglements. We pretend we know not in intimacy, but—perfectly, beautifully—in distance. We deny the legitimacy of knowledge born of love. While Augustine sees that temptation and paints its portrait more than once, the better wisdom he offers is the truth that no intelligibility comes apart from incarnate love, this side of the veil at least. The gaps and fractures in our attempts to speak with one another should prompt us to evaluate our sense of what moves us toward understanding or insight.

Augustine invites readers to acknowledge the connection between intelligibility and intimacy. Intimacy is charity tied to flesh. Meanings shared in the context of love take their vibrancy from the lives of those who express them. In memorializing his conversation with Adeodatus, Augustine displays a love not abstracted from bodies and places, nor guarded from alienation and heartbreak. That love draws father and son into understanding, beyond any meaning they might have assigned to happiness. Through the intimacy of their love, they are again and again drawn out of the womb of certainty and security and into the happy life. The beata vita is sometimes light and shining, sometimes dark and broken. *De magistro* reminds us that we enjoy the blessed life not through hewing to an impossibly inhuman standard of perfect wholeness. What we take to be brokenness is no mistake. It is a revelation, part of the very life of God.

Augustine's image of parturition in *De magistro* is, as we have said, a hint that the text is a spiritual exercise aimed at preparing its student to be delivered into the beata vita. Working through the temptation to think that we talk only to inform one another—and the contracted imagination for spirit and interiority that accompanies that conviction—is precisely what moves us into love of God and love of others. Attending to our problematic desire for the contraction of meaning can, over time, draw us out into the heat and light of the beata vita, a place where we can live. Augustine knows we often try to cling to that contraction—to live with it and in it, permanently, instead of letting ourselves be delivered out of our cramped way with words. But he reminds us that a real life with others awaits us. The beata vita is not what we imagine from our vantage within that strained and narrowed approach to meaning, where we work to master words and minds while shielding ourselves from loss. Augustine ushers us through that contraction so that we might be delivered into a life most blessed. His hope is not for safety or sterile perfection. Instead, Augustine's hope is for life, conceived as an offering of love. He remembers his beloved son in that hope, the hope of the Word made flesh.

NOTES

Introduction

1. Catherine Conybeare led the way with *The Irrational Augustine*. Other examples of this trend include Ian Clausen's *On Love, Confession, Surrender and the Moral Self*; Erik Kenyon's *Augustine and the Dialogue*; and Michael Foley's new translations of *Against the Academics, On the Happy Life, On Order*, and *Soliloquies*.

2. *mag.* 1.1 (CCL 29:157): "quid tibi uidemur efficere uelle, cum loquimur?" I use the CCL edition of *De magistro*, edited by K. D. Daur (1970), as my source for the Latin. In translating the text, I have benefited from consulting the translations of Peter King and Garry Wills. The former sticks strictly to the Latin, while the latter suggests the playfulness of the exchange. In my own translations, I have tried to walk a middle path. Translations of *De magistro* and *Confessiones* are mine, with exceptions noted.

3. See, for example, Burnyeat, "Wittgenstein and Augustine *De Magistro*"; King, "Augustine on the Impossibility of Teaching"; and Matthews, "Knowledge and Illumination."

4. When Augustine revisits *De magistro* in the *Retractationes*, he makes no mention of a theory of signs (*retr.* 1.12).

Chapter One

1. *mag.* 1.1 (CCL 29:157): "quid tibi uidemur efficere uelle, cum loquimur?"

2. In translations of *De magistro*, the words *docere* and *discere* have typically been translated as *to teach* and *to learn*, respectively. See, for example, Peter King's translation of *The Teacher*. In addition to rendering *docere* as *to teach* translators frequently translate *magister* as *teacher*, thereby eliding a difference present in the Latin.

While I prefer the terms *informing* and *being informed*, I will sometimes use *to teach* for *docere*, particularly when discussing scholarship that makes use of that term.

3. Carroll, "Jabberwocky," 219.

4. *mag.* 11.36 (CCL 29:194): "hactenus uerba ualuerunt, quibus ut plurimum tribuam, admonent tantum, ut quaeramus res, non exhibent, ut norimus. is me autem aliquid docet, qui uel oculis uel ulli corporis sensui uel ipsi etiam menti praebet ea, quae cognoscere uolo. uerbis igitur nisi uerba non discimus, immo sonitum strepitumque uerborum; nam si ea, quae signa non sunt, uerba esse non possunt, quamuis iam auditum uerbum nescio tamen uerbum esse, donec quid significet sciam."

5. Cloeren calls the dialogue a "transcendental investigation in Kant's sense," wherein Augustine tries to outline the conditions of the possibility of teaching and learning. Here the claim that we talk to teach or inform is never fundamentally questioned as a motivation but is instead reinforced. See Cloeren, "St. Augustine's De Magistro."

6. For examples, see Burnyeat, "Wittgenstein and Augustine *De Magistro*," on Christ's illumination of the mind; King, "Augustine on the Impossibility of Teaching"; Kirwan, "Augustine's Philosophy of Language"; Matthews, "Knowledge and Illumination"; and Mackey, "The Mediator Mediated," on Christ's clarification of ambiguities of reference.

7. *mag.* 11.38 (CCL 29:195–96): "de uniuersis autem, quae intellegimus, non loquentem, qui personat foris, sed intus ipsi menti praesidentem consulimus ueritatem, uerbis fortasse ut consulamus admoniti. ille autem, qui consulitur, docet, qui in interiore homine habitare dictus est Christus, id est incommutabilis dei uirtus atque sempiterna sapientia, quam quidem omnis rationalis anima consulit."

8. Schumacher, *Divine Illumination*, 58–59.

9. Schumacher, *Divine Illumination*, 60.

10. Mackey, "The Mediator Mediated," 141.

11. Wetzel sums up the worry in "The Oracle and the Inner Teacher," 287: "Augustine's identification of the inner teacher as Christ, 'the unending wisdom and changeless virtue of God' (11.38), is not likely to diminish the impression of his more naturalistically inclined readers that he has lapsed into religious enthusiasm (again). It can seem as if he is overreacting in *De magistro* to the limitations of any attempt to secure meaning ostensively."

12. King, "Augustine on the Impossibility of Teaching," 191.

13. A portion of my discussion of Burnyeat in this paragraph and the two following first appeared in my essay "The Drama of *De magistro*." I am grateful to Peeters Publishers for permission to use the material here, in reworked form.

14. Burnyeat, "Wittgenstein and Augustine *De Magistro*," 4. Burnyeat uses *teaching* for *docere*.

15. Burnyeat, "Wittgenstein and Augustine *De Magistro*," 4.

16. Burnyeat, "Wittgenstein and Augustine *De Magistro*," 15.

17. Burnyeat concludes his piece with a quotation from the *Investigations*: "Would it not be possible for us, however, to calculate as we actually do (all agreeing, and so on), and still at every step to have a feeling of being guided by the rules as by a spell, feeling astonishment at the fact that we agreed? (We might give thanks to the Deity for our agreement.)" It is curious that Burnyeat chooses this passage—with its odd mention of giving thanks to the Deity for our agreement—as his way of gesturing toward Wittgenstein's naturalistic explanation. See Burnyeat, "Wittgenstein and Augustine *De Magistro*," 16–17, and Wittgenstein, *Philosophical Investigations*, §234.

18. Burnyeat, "Wittgenstein and Augustine *De Magistro*," 16. Cloeren takes an opposite approach, accepting the split between philosophy and theology, while choosing to embrace Augustine's theological solutions. Cloeren writes that Augustine's method in *De magistro* is "transcendental and includes language critical elements. His answers to philosophical problems, however, remain ultimately theological and biblical." Cloeren, "St. Augustine's De Magistro," 27.

19. James Wetzel examines the naturalist's temptation in reading *De magistro* and ties it to the assumption "that all of Augustine's beloveds lose out in the end to the original goodness that has no further use for them but use" ("The Oracle and the Inner Teacher," 291). While he finds limitations in Burnyeat's reading, Wetzel does not abandon naturalism altogether. Instead he develops what he terms a "piecemeal naturalism," a naturalism neither tragic nor secular. See his essay "The Oracle and the Inner Teacher."

20. At the close of his reading of *De magistro* as "Augustine's most inviting presentation of his philosophy of language," Matthews concludes that contemporary innatist theories of language can be spoken in Augustine's terms, if the specifical theological content is shed. See Matthews, *Augustine*, 25.

21. See Matthews, *Augustine*, 32.

22. Cary, *Outward Signs*, 96.

23. Cary, *Outward Signs*, 88.

24. Cary, *Outward Signs*, 89.

25. Cary, *Outward Signs*, 99.

26. Cary, *Outward Signs*, 99.

27. Cary, *Outward Signs*, 99.

28. Cary, *Augustine's Invention of the Inner Self*, 50.

29. Cary says the conclusion of the dialogue is "in effect a gesture of profound renunciation." Cary, *Outward Signs*, 91.

30. This is where Cary finds he must take his leave from Augustine. Cary wants incarnation. He thinks external things matter—particularly when it comes to matters of faith.

31. See Mendelson, "By the Things Themselves."

32. Mendelson, "By the Things Themselves," 487.

33. Mendelson, "By the Things Themselves," 489.

34. Wittgenstein, *Philosophical Investigations*, §36. "Wo unsere Sprache uns einen Körper vermuten läßt, und kein Körper ist, dort, möchten wir sagen, sei ein *Geist*."

35. Ann Clark is unusual and perceptive in suggesting that the acceptance of the claim that we talk to teach might be a seduction in which the reader accepts more than meets the eye. See Clark, "Unity and Method."

36. Readers who overlook Augustine's shift away from giving an account of how words facilitate teaching/informing will have a hard time making sense of early passages in the dialogue. Christopher Kirwan's consideration of *De magistro* in his article on Augustine's philosophy of language suffers considerably from a neglect of the context in which remarks were made. See Kirwan, "Augustine's Philosophy of Language." Nothing in the first part of *De magistro* should be taken as Augustine's considered view. The text is, after all, a dialogue, full of twists and reversals. Frederick Crosson and Goulven Madec offer helpful orientation to the structure of the dialogue in Crosson, "Structure of the *De magistro*," and Madec, "Analyse du *De magistro*." An even more ambitious guide and commentary, with attention to Augustine's Stoic inheritance and *De magistro*'s relevance to post-Wittgensteinian philosophy of language, can be found in Bermon, *La signification et l'enseignement*.

37. Matthews, "Knowledge and Illumination," 173.

38. *mag.* 1.2 (CCL 29:159): "quare non opus est locutione, cum oramus, id est sonantibus uerbis, nisi forte, sicut sacerdotes faciunt, significandae mentis suae causa, non ut deus, sed ut homines audiant et consensione quadam per commemorationem suspendantur in deum."

39. According to Cary's Augustine, external words can only be directed "horizontally, as it were, from one human being to another. The will of the heart raised inwardly to God is true prayer, and this will says literally nothing. It is turned inward and therefore seeks God free of external things like words." Cary, *Outward Signs*, 93.

40. Wetzel, *Parting Knowledge*, 111.

41. Teubner suggests that Augustine draws here on Ambrose's language about prayer in *De sacramentis*. See Teubner, *Prayer after Augustine*, 44–49. Teubner finds in *De magistro* "outlines of a unique theory and practice of prayer" (45).

42. Sessa, "Christianity and the Cubiculum," 177.

43. Sessa, "Christianity and the Cubiculum," 180.

44. Sessa, "Christianity and the Cubiculum," 181.

45. Sessa, "Christianity and the Cubiculum," 182.

46. Wittgenstein, *Philosophical Investigations*, §19.

Chapter Two

1. While Augustine relies here on the Stoic view that all words signify, Rist argues this moment reflects a departure from Stoic theory, which holds that a proposition *as a whole* also signifies. If Augustine and Adeodatus were strictly following a Stoic account, they would have identified nine signs here. See Rist, *Augustine*, 26–27 and 314–16.

2. *mag.* 2.3 (CCL 29:160): "'nihil' quid aliud significat, nisi id quod non est?"

3. *mag.* 2.3 (CCL 29:160): "uerum fortasse dicis, sed reuocat me ab assentiendo, quod superius concessisti non esse signum, nisi aliquid significet; quod autem non est, nullo modo esse aliquid potest. quare secundum uerbum in hoc uersu non est signum, quia non significat aliquid, et falso inter nos constitit, quod omnia uerba signa sint aut omne signum aliquid significet."

4. *mag.* 2.3 (CCL 29:160): "nimis quidem urges, sed quando non habemus quid significemus, omnino stulte uerbum aliquod promimus; tu autem nunc mecum loquendo credo quod nullum sonum frustra emittis, sed omnibus, quae ore tuo erumpunt, signum mihi das, ut aliquid intellegam. quapropter non te oportet istas duas syllabas enuntiare dum loqueris, si per eas non significas quicquam. si autem uides necessariam per eas enuntiationem fieri nosque doceri uel commoneri, cum auribus insonant, uides etiam profecto, quid uelim dicere, sed explicare non possum."

5. *mag.* 2.3 (CCL 29:161): "ridiculum hoc quidem est."

6. I first explored some of these ideas about the connection between Augustine and Virgil in an essay titled, "Making Sense of Virgil in *De magistro*."

7. Vergil, *Aeneid*, 2.12–13. I use Sarah Ruden's gorgeous translation of *The Aeneid*. For Virgil's Latin, I use Mynor's *P. Vergili Maronis Opera*.

8. Vergil, *Aeneid*, 2.659–67.

9. Vergil, *Aeneid*, 2.677–78.

10. In her masterful study of Augustine's engagement with Virgil, Sabine MacCormack suggests that Troy may be a metaphor for the view of language Augustine is about to take down. See MacCormack, *Shadows of Poetry*, 58.

11. "One wonders if, perhaps, the quotation from Virgil is not somehow self-referential, i.e. if somehow it does not describe Augustine the author's own

situation." Kries, "Virgil, Daniel, and Augustine's Dialogic Pedagogy in *De Magis-tro*," 148. Kries indicates several parallels between this scene in the *Aeneid* and the story of Augustine's life. In particular, he suggests that Monica, prevented from returning to Africa by her death, is perhaps meant to be a Creusa.

12. Vergil, *Aeneid*, 2.789–91.

13. Though many note the oddity of the rhetorician's contraction of the function of words, few commentators try to uncover the reason for it. See, for example, Stead, "Review of John Rist's *Augustine*," 320: "By neglecting the distinctive functions of words that are not nouns Augustine rules out *ab initio* any satisfactory theory of the sentence."

14. Catherine Atherton maps out the positions in her clear and comprehensive work on the Stoic concept of ambiguity. See her *Stoics on Ambiguity*, 298–310. For a different take on the passage from *De magistro*, see Nawar, "Every Word Is a Name."

15. Describing the dearth of surviving literature on Stoic ambiguity, Atherton comments, "The most unexpected source is perhaps St Augustine of Hippo, who provides evidence, of immense value despite its indirectness, about one of the most important strands in Stoic work on ambiguity, that relating to autonymy or linguistic reflexivity." Augustine's *On Dialectic* and *On the Teacher*, she continues, "together suggest the probable explanation of Chrysippus' thesis that 'every word is by nature ambiguous': every word is also its own name." *Stoics on Ambiguity*, 37–38.

16. The philosopher Ludwig Wittgenstein takes up a similar point in his engagement with Augustine's portrait of his infant self in *Confessiones* 1. In the opening of his *Philosophical Investigations*, Wittgenstein says Augustine's picture contains the roots of this idea (§1): "Every word has a meaning. This meaning is correlated with the word. It is the object for which the word stands." For a detailed look at the terms of Wittgenstein's engagement with Augustine on this point, see Affeldt, "Being Lost and Finding Home"; Cavell, "Availability of Wittgenstein's Later Philosophy," in *Must We Mean*, 44–72; Eldridge, *Leading a Human Life*; Kidd, "In the Beginning": Mulhall, *Philosophical Myths*; and Wetzel, "Wittgenstein's Augustine: The Inauguration of the Later Philosophy," in *Parting Knowledge*, 225–47.

17. Atherton, *Stoics on Ambiguity*, 274.

18. See Wittgenstein, *Philosophical Investigations*, §55ff.

19. My comments here are not a criticism of Stoic theory. The temptation related to the name thesis draws on the rest of the concerns raised by Augustine in *De magistro*.

20. In his translation of *De magistro* in *Saint Augustine's Childhood*, Garry Wills translates the question into English as "whether the masculine is masculine" and does so for good reason—the need to have a multisyllabic word so that it can be broken down into parts. The tone is perhaps more teasing when the original word *man* is

retained. The reader should recall that Latin has neither definite nor indefinite articles, so the translation "whether the masculine is masculine" does not reflect the identity of "homo homo"; this arguably changes how the question would be taken.

21. Irigaray worries about philosophers' preoccupation with finding names for meanings while neglecting the relationship between the speaking subjects. She laments the world of difference between speaking with the other and naming. See Irigaray, *The Way of Love*, 7. She suggests that philosophy has neglected the relationship between speaking subjects in favor of inquiry into subject and object or subject and what he tries to say. The philosophical tradition has therefore left individual subjects in isolation from each other. She writes, "If man is the animal endowed with language, who could imagine that this property serves simply to express his needs and to name the object of his world? Does not language have to serve for transforming instincts and needs into shared desires?" Irigaray, *The Way of Love*, 39.

22. *mag.* 8.21 (CCL 29:180): "sed quonam tantis ambagibus tecum peruenire moliar, difficile dictu est hoc loco. tu enim fortasse aut ludere nos et a seriis rebus auocare animum quasi quibusdam puerilibus quaestiunculis arbitraris aut paruam uel mediocrem aliquam utilitatem requirere aut, si magnum quiddam parturire istam disputationem suspicaris, iamiamque id scire siue saltem audire desideras. ego autem credas uelim neque me uilia ludicra hoc instituisse sermone, quamuis fortasse ludamus, idque ipsum tamen non puerili sensu aestimandum sit, neque parua bona uel mediocria cogitare. et tamen, si dicam uitam esse quandam beatam eandemque sempiternam, quo nos deo duce id est ipsa ueritate gradibus quibusdam infirmo gressui nostro accomodatis perduci cupiam, uereor, ne ridiculus uidear, qui non rerum ipsarum, quae significantur, sed signorum consideratione tantam uiam ingredi coeperim. dabis igitur ueniam, si praeludo tecum non ludendi gratia, sed exercendi uires et mentis aciem, quibus regionis illius, ubi beata uita est, calorem ac lucem non modo sustinere, uerum et amare possimus."

Chapter Three

1. Augustine hints at this point in *De magistro*. It can be seen every more clearly in *Confessiones* 1. I sketch the portrait of Augustine's infant-informer of *Confessiones* 1 in my essay "In the Beginning."

2. Irigaray, *Marine Lover*, 3.

3. Irigaray, *Marine Lover*, 3.

4. Irigaray, *Speculum*, 142.

5. Irigaray, *This Sex Which Is Not One*, 78.

6. "The ideal reply to her writing, she says explicitly, is 'who are you?'— the address is to the other. What she wants to do is to 'bring about a change in

discourse.' This would account, I think, for the extraordinary variety of responses that she elicits—to this extent she has succeeded in her aim, for the interlocutor/reader is often forced to put him/herself into play in order to read her enigmatic texts, and the response is often as much to do with the reader as with Irigaray. At its best, it is a creative response in which there is a productive interaction between reader and text." Whitford, "Introduction," 14.

7. Oliver, "Reading Nietzsche with Irigaray," 50.

8. Oliver, "Reading Nietzsche with Irigaray," 52–53.

9. Nietzsche describes the basic hostility to life he perceives in Christian teaching: "Christianity was from the beginning, essentially and fundamentally, life's nausea and disgust with life, merely concealed behind, masked by, dressed up as, faith in 'another' or 'better' life. Hatred of 'the world,' condemnations of the passions, fear of beauty and sensuality, a beyond invented the better to slander this life, at bottom a craving for the nothing." Nietzsche, "Birth of Tragedy," 23.

10. Irigaray, *Marine Lover*, 127.

11. Irigaray, *Marine Lover*, 124.

12. Irigaray, *Marine Lover*, 129.

13. Irigaray, *Marine Lover*, 125.

14. Irigaray, *Marine Lover*, 131.

15. Irigaray, *Marine Lover*, 136.

16. Irigaray, *Marine Lover*, 130.

17. One might hear an echo of the story of the Tower of Babel, where the human beings apparently see no gift in the fact of their living and speaking together. Instead they value and seek only divine recognition, the acknowledgment of the divine Father.

18. Irigaray, *Marine Lover*, 142.

19. Irigaray, *Marine Lover*, 129.

20. Irigaray, *Marine Lover*, 131.

21. Irigaray, *Marine Lover*, 138.

22. Irigaray, *Marine Lover*, 141.

23. Irigaray, *Marine Lover*, 142.

24. Irigaray, *Marine Lover*, 139.

25. Irigaray, *Marine Lover*, 138.

26. Irigaray, *Marine Lover*, 144.

27. Irigaray, *Marine Lover*, 145–46. Italics mine.

28. Irigaray, *Marine Lover*, 157.

29. Irigaray, *Marine Lover*, 153.

30. Irigaray, *Marine Lover*, 158.

31. Irigaray, *Marine Lover*, 156.

32. Irigaray, *Marine Lover*, 157.

33. Irigaray, *Marine Lover*, 148.

34. Irigaray, *Marine Lover*, 164.

35. This anxiety, translated into a mundane context (mortal father and mortal son), is a recurrent theme in Stanley Cavell's autobiography *Little Did I Know*.

36. Irigaray, *Marine Lover*, 165.

37. Irigaray, *Marine Lover*, 166.

38. Irigaray, *Marine Lover*, 166.

39. Irigaray, *Marine Lover*, 165.

40. Irigaray, *Marine Lover*, 169.

Chapter Four

1. "*Intermezzo*: From the Book on the Nature of Things," in Hinsey, *White Fire of Time*, 28.

2. *mag.* 8.21 (CCL 29:180): "dabis igitur ueniam, si praeludo tecum non ludendi gratia, sed exercendi uires et mentis aciem, quibus regionis illius, ubi beata uita est, calorem ac lucem non modo sustinere, uerum et amare possimus."

3. Michael Mendelson tries to make something of the comments about the beata vita (he terms this passage the "eudaimonistic interlude"), but, on his account, one's soul has first to make a long trek through the "grim landscape" of embodiment—and the prospect of making one's home in the beata vita seems dim. See Mendelson, "By the Things Themselves," as well as two other essays that mark the beata vita comments as significant: Clark, "Unity and Method," and Crosson, "Structure of the *De Magistro*."

4. *De magistro* was written in 389, *Confessiones* between 397 and 401. The two projects were written with different aims in mind, and the latter was written by a man changed by time and distance from the events recorded. Nonetheless, strong resonances exist between the texts.

5. *conf.* 7.7.11: "quae illa tormenta parturientis cordis mei, qui gemitus, deus meus!" My source for the Latin is O'Donnell's edition. Translations of the Latin are mine, except where noted. I benefited from consulting both the Chadwick and Boulding translations.

6. *conf.* 7.10.16: "qui nouit ueritatem, nouit eam, et qui nouit eam, nouit aeternitatem; caritas nouit eam."

7. *conf.* 7.10.16: "cibus sum grandium: cresce et manducabis me. nec tu me in te mutabis sicut cibum carnis tuae, sed tu mutaberis in me." I cannot improve on Wetzel's translation here. Wetzel, *Augustine*, 56.

8. Wetzel, "Body Double," 74.

9. John Freccero finds in this passage the notion that sin, for Augustine, is a principle of individuation. If the self is distinctive because of sin, it is hard to imagine how an individual could ever get close to God. See Freccero, "Autobiography and Narrative."

10. Wetzel, "Body Double," 74.

11. I first explored some of these ideas—the breakdown of intimacy in *Confessiones* 7 and the forms of intimacy in *Confessiones* 8—in an essay published in *Ramify*: "Parting Words: Augustine on Love and Loss." There, I tie these episodes to Augustine's failure of love in *Confessiones* 4, and I argue that the *Confessiones* can be read as a meditation on intimacy.

12. See Courcelle's discussion of the "vaines tentatives d'extases plotiniennes" in his *Recherches Sur Les Confessions*, 157–67. Following him, one consensus reading has been that the abortive contemplative ascents of *Confessiones* 7 are followed by the successful achievement of Plotinian ecstasy at Ostia—once Augustine has embraced a more ascetic life. For a brief discussion of whether the Plotinian ascent was meant to be permanent (as opposed to frustrated and limited), see O'Donnell, *Augustine's Confessions*, vol. 2, 435–37.

13. See Skerrett, "Consuetudo Carnalis."

14. Skerrett, "Consuetudo Carnalis," 500.

15. Skerrett, "Consuetudo Carnalis," 499.

16. Skerrett, "Consuetudo Carnalis," 497.

17. Skerrett, "Consuetudo Carnalis," 497.

18. Skerrett, "Consuetudo Carnalis," 497.

19. *conf.* 7.20.26: "inter uidentes quo eundum sit nec uidentes qua, et uiam ducentem ad beatificam patriam non tantum cernendam sed et habitandam."

20. *conf.* 7.19.25: "quid autem sacramenti haberet uerbum caro factum, ne suspicari quidem poteram."

21. *conf.* 8.5.11: "ego autem adhuc terra obligatus militare tibi recusabam et impedimentis omnibus sic timebam expediri, quemadmodum impediri timendum est."

22. *conf.* 8.7.18: "quae non in me dixi? quibus sententiarum uerberibus non flagellaui animam meam, ut sequeretur me conantem post te ire? et renitebatur, recusabat, et non se excusabat."

23. *conf.* 1.14.23: "nulla enim uerba illa noueram, et saeuis terroribus ac poenis ut nossem instabatur mihi uehementer."

24. *conf.* 1.14.23: "nam et Latina aliquando infans utique nulla noueram, et tamen aduertendo didici sine ullo metu atque cruciatu, inter etiam blandimenta nutricum et ioca adridentium et laetitias adludentium."

25. *conf.* 8.11.27: "proice te in eum! noli metuere. non se subtrahet ut cadas."

26. This line of argument is uncommon. F. B. A. Asiedu makes a compelling case. See Asiedu, "Example of a Woman." Virginia Burrus, Mark D. Jordan, and Karmen MacKendrick read the scene quite differently, writing that Continence "is the opposite of the unnamed and all too fleshly 'mistress' we have seen torn from Augustine's side." *Seducing Augustine*, 55.

27. For a moving portrait of the couple, see Shanzer, "Avulsa a Latere Meo."

28. While I have been supplying my own translations throughout, here I rely on Chadwick's rendering. Most translations of the *Confessions* make the verse sound more body-denying than the Latin requires (*conf.* 8.12.29): "non in comessationibus et ebrietatibus, non in cubilibus et impudicitiis, non in contentione et aemulatione, sed induite dominum Iesum Christum et carnis providentiam ne feceritis in concupiscentiis." Wetzel's translation—which I give shortly—better reflects the fact that Augustine's problem is not his flesh, but his habitual ways of trying to care for that flesh, ways that reinforce its seeming neediness.

29. I am indebted to Wetzel's attention to this detail of the text. He suggests the voice may have reminded Augustine of his life with his son. It may also have prompted him to remember Christ's own need for parenting. See Wetzel, *Augustine*, 103–4.

30. Wetzel, *Parting Knowledge*, 98. Cf. *conf.* 8.12.29.

31. Wetzel, *Augustine*, 105.

32. Wetzel, *Augustine*, 104.

33. For a beautiful reflection on this point, see Marion, *In the Self's Place*. He reminds his reader that it is not simply natal life that is gifted, but also the beata vita.

34. One might think here of the wedding feast at Cana where Mary directs her son to act, though he says his time has not yet come.

35. *mag.* 8.21 (CCL 29:180): "et tamen, si dicam uitam esse quandam beatam eandemque sempiternam, quo nos deo duce id est ipsa ueritate gradibus quibusdam infirmo gressui nostro accomodatis perduci cupiam, uereor, ne ridiculus uidear, qui non rerum ipsarum, quae significantur, sed signorum consideratione tantam uiam ingredi coeperim."

36. *conf.* 1.14.23: "didici uero illa sine poenali onere urgentium, cum me urgeret cor meum ad parienda concepta sua, et qua non esset, nisi aliqua uerba didicissem non a docentibus sed a loquentibus, in quorum et ego auribus parturiebam quidquid sentiebam."

37. *mag.* 8.21 (CCL 29:180): "dabis igitur ueniam, si praeludo tecum non ludendi gratia, sed exercendi uires et mentis aciem, quibus regionis illius, ubi beata uita est, calorem ac lucem non modo sustinere, uerum et amare possimus."

Chapter Five

1. Adam Ployd suggests a line of continuity between Augustine's early discussion of Christ the teacher in *De magistro* and Augustine's discussion of Christ the Word in later works such as *De trinitate*. He is emphatic about the theological substance of *De magistro*. See his "The Place of *De magistro*."

2. "Loves: Magdalene's Epistle," in Cairns, *Recovered Body*, 68.

3. Irigaray, *Marine Lover*, 173.

4. Irigaray, *Marine Lover*, 174.

5. Irigaray, *Marine Lover*, 173.

6. Irigaray, *Marine Lover*, 174.

7. Irigaray, *Marine Lover*, 175.

8. Irigaray, *Marine Lover*, 176.

9. Irigaray, *Marine Lover*, 172.

10. Martini and Mimmi, *Annunciation*.

11. "Loves: Magdalene's Epistle," in Cairns, *Recovered Body*, 64–65, 67.

12. "Loves: Magdalene's Epistle," in Cairns, *Recovered Body*, 68.

13. "East Coker," Eliot, *Four Quartets*, ll. 112–13.

14. "East Coker," Eliot *Four Quartets*, ll. 123–24.

15. Irigaray, *Marine Lover*, 169.

16. Irigaray, *Marine Lover*, 169.

17. Irigaray, *Marine Lover*, 169.

18. Irigaray, *Marine Lover*, 176.

19. Irigaray, *Marine Lover*, 176.

20. Irigaray, *Marine Lover*, 177.

21. Irigaray, *Marine Lover*, 181.

22. Irigaray, *Marine Lover*, 182.

23. Irigaray, *Marine Lover*, 182.

24. Irigaray, *Marine Lover*, 73.

25. Irigaray, *Marine Lover*, 73.

26. Irigaray, *Marine Lover*, 186.

Chapter Six

1. The bird catcher example anticipates the *Confessiones* 10 scene where Augustine silently asks the creatures of the whole created order who made them: "My question was my attention, and their answer their beauty." *conf.* 10.6.9: "interrogatio mea intentio mea et responsio eorum species eorum."

2. *mag.* 10.33 (CCL 29:192): "cum enim mihi signum datur, si nescientem me inuenerit, cuius rei signum sit, docere me nihil potest, si uero scientem, quid disco per signum?"

3. *mag.* 10.33 (CCL 29:192): "ita magis signum re cognita quam signo dato ipsa res discitur."

4. *mag.* 10.34 (CCL 29:193): "potius enim ut dixi uim uerbi, id est significationem, quae latet in sono, re ipsa, quae significatur, cognita discimus, quam illam tali significatione percipimus."

5. *mag.* 10.35 (CCL 29:194): "non enim, cum rem ipsam didici, uerbis alienis credidi, sed oculis meis; illis tamen fortasse ut adtenderem credidi, id es ut aspectu quaererem, quid uiderem." I diverge from CCL, in taking "oculis" for "oculus." In doing so, I follow Emmanuel Bermon's Latin text in *La signification et l'enseignement*, as well as the Latin text in *De magistro / Der Lehrer*.

6. *mag.* 11.36 (CCL 29:194): "hactenus uerba ualuerunt, quibus ut plurimum tribuam, admonent tantum, ut quaeramus res, non exhibent, ut norimus. is me autem aliquid docet, qui uel oculis uel ulli corporis sensui uel ipsi etiam menti praebet ea, quae cognoscere uolo. uerbis igitur nisi uerba non discimus, immo sonitum strepitumque uerborum; nam si ea, quae signa non sunt, uerba esse non possunt, quamuis iam auditum uerbum nescio tamen uerbum esse, donec quid significet sciam."

7. We might dispute, for example, whether the young men's confidence and peace as they entered the furnace was faith or madness.

8. *mag.* 11.38 (CCL 29:195–96): "de uniuersis autem, quae intellegimus, non loquentem, qui personat foris, sed intus ipsi menti praesidentem consulimus ueritatem, uerbis fortasse ut consulamus admoniti. ille autem, qui consulitur, docet, qui in interiore homine habitare dictus est Christus, id est incommutabilis dei uirtus atque sempiterna sapientia, quam quidem omnis rationalis anima consulit, sed tantum cuique panditur, quantum capere propter propriam siue malum siue bonam uoluntatem potest. et si quando fallitur non fit uitio consultae ueritatis, ut neque huius, quae foris est, lucis uitium est, quod corporei oculi saepe falluntur, quam lucem de rebus uisibilibus consuli fatemur, ut eas nobis, quantum cernere ualemus, ostendat."

9. *mag.* 12.40 (CCL 29:198): "uelut si abs te quaererem hoc ipsum quod agitur, utrumnam uerbis doceri nihil possit, et absurdum tibi primo uideretur non ualenti totum conspicere, sic ergo quaerere oportuit, ut tuae sese uires habent ad audiendum illum intus magistrum."

10. *mag.* 14.46 (CCL 29:202): "nunc enim ne plus eis quam oportet tribueremus, admonui te, ut iam non crederemus tantum, sed etiam intellegere

inciperemus, quam uere scriptum sit auctoritate diuina, ne nobis quemquam magistrum dicamus in terris, quod unus omnium magister in caelis sit."

11. *mag.* 14.46 (CCL 29:202–3): "quid sit autem in caelis, docebit ipse, a quo etiam per homines signis admonemur foris, ut ad eum intro conuersi erudiamur, quem diligere ac nosse beata uita est, quam se omnes clamant quaerere, pauci autem sunt, qui eam uere se inuenisse laetentur."

12. Wills's translation of Adeodatus's final speech suggests that words merely afford an opportunity for Christ to do the real work of informing minds: "By the occasion your words provided, I have learned that words can do no more than provide such an occasion for learning; that words cannot even tell us much about the thoughts of those using them, and that their truth is to be established only by our internal teacher, who provides external words only as an occasion for me to love him more ardently, with his help, and learn in proportion as I love" (*mag.* 14.46). Describing words as the external occasion for us to submit to the internal schooling of Christ devalues signs and human use of them. It does not fit with the conversation on display in *De magistro*.

13. *mag.* 14.46 (CCL 29:203): "quem iam fauente ipso tanto ardentius diligam, quanto ero in discendo prouectior."

14. Vaught, *Encounters with God*, 126.

15. Camille Bennett briefly suggests that there is a parallel between this conversation at Ostia and the last conversation between Aeneas and his father in the underworld. See her "The Conversion of Vergil," 65.

16. *conf.* 9.10.24: "erigentes nos ardentiore affectu in idipsum, perambulauimus gradatim cuncta corporalia et ipsum caelum, unde sol et luna et stellae lucent super terram."

17. While the dominating metaphor of the *Confessiones* 7 experience is that of vision, the dominating metaphor of the *Confessiones* 9 experience is that of touch (*attingere*), a metaphor connoting something more immediate, intimate, and bodily.

18. *conf.* 9.10.24: "et ibi uita sapientia est, per quam fiunt omnia ista, et quae fuerunt et quae futura sunt, et ipsa non fit, sed sic est ut fuit, et sic erit semper."

19. *conf.* 9.9.21: "docente te magistro intimo in schola pectoris."

20. Vaught, *Encounters with God*, 128.

21. John Peter Kenney observes, "Augustine's rhetorical training is never more effective, nor so hidden from view." See Kenney, *Mysticism of Saint Augustine*, 78.

22. Vaught, *Encounters with God*, 129: "Though the infinite richness of truth allows Augustine and Monica to remain in its presence for only a moment, they are able to return to it by participating in a conversation in which figurative language expresses what literal language about the relation between God and the soul

can never say. Both Monica and Augustine have embraced the incarnation as the middle term that binds God and the soul together; and as a consequence, the incarnated language they speak on this occasion places them in the middle ground between God and the soul, where they express the richness of God in the figurative discourse appropriate to it."

23. Augustine surely knows that those who do not know or do not believe in Christ are able to speak meaningfully with each other. He seems to suggest, however, that the deepest wells of meaning are only available to those in relationship with Christ. Without that relationship to the Word, human words will fall short, no matter how useful they may be.

24. Wetzel, *Augustine*, 111: "Augustine and Adeodatus conclude that they do share an inner life together, one that neither of them possesses separately. They call this life their teacher. This is the life that both begins and ends their life's argument, allowing them learning through the hesitations, sometimes terrible, of sin."

Chapter Seven

1. Wetzel mentions several possible explanations: "Perhaps she did so because she loved Adeodatus and wanted him to have more opportunities in life. Perhaps she loved Augustine and wanted him to get to know his son better. Perhaps she loved them both and couldn't abide the thought of their separation. There are other possibilities, of course, most of them more cynical." *Augustine*, 100.

2. Wills proposes that Augustine may have moved Adeodatus to Thagaste to allow the boy to live near his mother. *Saint Augustine's Childhood*, 127.

3. *conf.* 9.6.14: "ingenio praeueniebat multos graues et doctos uiros."

4. Wills explains: "Augustine's practice in these early dialogues was to carry on a real discussion, taken down by stenographers, and then to polish the resulting text. He assures us . . . that all the responses (*sensa*) made by Godsend [i.e., Adeodatus] in this published work were actually voiced by him in the original conversation. Given Augustine's scrupulous standard of truthfulness, we can assume that he edited Godsend's words very lightly, preserving their point." *Saint Augustine's Childhood*, 127–28.

5. *conf.* 9.6.14: "horrori mihi erat illud ingenium. et quis praeter te talium miraculorum opifex?"

6. *conf.* 9.6.14: "munera tua tibi confiteor, domine deus meus, creator omnium et multum potens formare nostra deformia, nam ego in illo puero praeter delictum non habebam."

7. See Bermon's notes on timing in *La signification et l'enseignement*, 21–22.

8. It is not, of course, impossible to give directions to a stranger at a bus stop. Those are not typically our most meaningful exchanges. In the rare case that they are, a richer context informs that exchange. Such rich contexts can develop quite quickly and derive from some shared experience.

9. Gregory, *Politics and the Order of Love*, 252.

10. This realization governs much of Wittgenstein's efforts in the *Philosophical Investigations*.

11. Beckett, *Endgame*, 61.

12. *conf.* 4.11.17: "et non uis utique stare syllabas sed transuolare, ut aliae ueniant et totum audias."

13. I develop this point in my essay "Book IV: Fugitive Beauty," 85–90.

BIBLIOGRAPHY

Affeldt, Steven G. "Being Lost and Finding Home: Philosophy, Confession, Recollection, and Conversion in Augustine's Confessions and Wittgenstein's Philosophical Investigations." In *Wittgenstein Reading*, edited by Sascha Bru, Wolfgang Huemer, and Daniel Steuer, 5–22. Berlin: De Gruyter, 2013.

Asiedu, F. B. A. "Following the Example of a Woman: Augustine's Conversion to Christianity in 386." *Vigiliae Christianae* 57 (2003): 276–306.

Atherton, Catherine. *The Stoics on Ambiguity*. Cambridge: Cambridge University Press, 1993.

Augustine. *Against the Academics*. Translated by Michael Foley. New Haven, CT: Yale University Press, 2019.

———. *Confessions: Text and Commentary*, edited by James J. O'Donnell. 3 vols. Oxford: Oxford University Press, 2013.

———. *Confessions*. Translated by Maria Boulding. New York: New City Press, 2014.

———. *Confessions*. Translated by Henry Chadwick. Oxford: Oxford University Press, 2008.

———. *De magistro*, edited by K. D. Daur. CCL 29. Turnholt: Brepols, 1970.

———. *De magistro / Der Lehrer*, edited by Peter Schulthess, Rudolf Rohrbach, and Therese Fuhrer. Augustinus Opera Werke. Paderborn, Germany: Ferdinand Schöningh, 2002.

———. *On the Happy Life*. Translated by Michael Foley. New Haven, CT: Yale University Press, 2019.

———. *On Order*. Translated by Michael Foley. New Haven, CT: Yale University Press, 2020.

———. *Retractationes*, edited by A. Mutzenbecher. CCL 57. Turnholt: Brepols, 1984.

———. *Saint Augustine's Childhood*, edited and translated by Garry Wills. New York: Viking, 2001.

———. *Soliloquies*. Translated by Michael Foley. New Haven, CT: Yale University Press, 2020.

———. *The Teacher*. Translated by Peter King. Indianapolis: Hackett, 1995.

Beckett, Samuel. *Endgame*. New York: Grove Press, 2009.

Bennett, Camille. "The Conversion of Vergil: The Aeneid in Augustine's Confessions." *Revue d'Études Augustiniennes et Patristiques* 34 (1988): 47–69.

Bermon, Emmanuel, and Saint Augustine. *La signification et l'enseignement: texte latin, traduction française et commentaire du* De magistro *de saint Augustin*. Paris: J. Vrin, 2007.

Burnyeat, Myles. "Wittgenstein and Augustine De Magistro." In *Augustine and Wittgenstein*, edited by John Doody et al., 1–20. Lanham, MD: Lexington Books, 2018.

Burrus, Virginia, Mark D. Jordan, and Karmen MacKendrick. *Seducing Augustine: Bodies, Desires, Confessions*. New York: Fordham University Press, 2010.

Cairns, Scott. *Recovered Body*. 2nd ed. Wichita, KS: Eighth Day Press, 2003.

Carroll, Lewis. "Jabberwocky." In *The Rattle Bag*, edited by Seamus Heaney and Ted Hughes, 219. London: Faber and Faber, 1982.

Cary, Phillip. *Augustine's Invention of the Inner Self: The Legacy of a Christian Platonist*. Oxford: Oxford University Press, 2000.

———. *Outward Signs: The Powerlessness of External Things in Augustine's Thought*. Oxford: Oxford University Press, 2008.

Cavell, Stanley. *Little Did I Know: Excerpts from Memory*. Stanford, CA: Stanford University Press, 2010.

———. *Must We Mean What We Say?* Cambridge: Cambridge University Press, 2002.

Clark, Ann. "Unity and Method in Augustine's De Magistro." *Augustinian Studies* 8 (1977): 1–10.

Clausen, Ian. *On Love, Confession, Surrender and the Moral Self*. New York: Bloomsbury, 2018.

Cloeren, Herman. "St. Augustine's De Magistro: A Transcendental Investigation." *Augustinian Studies* 16 (1985): 21–27.

Conybeare, Catherine. *The Irrational Augustine*. Oxford: Oxford University Press, 2006.

Courcelle, Pierre. *Recherches Sur Les Confessions de Saint Augustin*. 2nd ed. Paris: de Boccard, 1968.

Crosson, Frederick. "The Structure of the *De magistro*." *Revue d'Études Augustiniennes et Patristiques* 35 (1989): 120–27.

Eldridge, Richard. *Leading a Human Life: Wittgenstein, Intentionality, and Romanticism*. Chicago: University of Chicago Press, 1997.

Eliot, T. S. *Four Quartets*. London: Faber and Faber, 1959.

Freccero, John. "Autobiography and Narrative." In *Reconstructing Individualism: Autonomy, Individuality, and the Self in Western Thought*, edited by Thomas C. Heller, Morton Sosna, and David E. Wellbery, 16–29. Stanford, CA: Stanford University Press, 1986.

Gregory, Eric. *Politics and the Order of Love*. Chicago: University of Chicago Press, 2008.

Hinsey, Ellen. *The White Fire of Time*. Middletown, CT: Wesleyan University Press, 2002.

Irigaray, Luce. *Marine Lover of Friedrich Nietzsche*. Translated by Gillian C. Gill. New York: Columbia University Press, 1991.

———. *Speculum of the Other Woman*. Translated by Gillian C. Gill. Ithaca, NY: Cornell University Press, 1985.

———. *This Sex Which Is Not One*. Translated by Catherine Porter. Ithaca, NY: Cornell University Press, 1985.

———. *The Way of Love*. Translated by Heidi Bostic and Stephen Pluháček. London: Continuum, 2002.

Kenney, John Peter. *The Mysticism of Saint Augustine: Rereading the Confessions*. New York: Routledge, 2005.

Kenyon, Erik. *Augustine and the Dialogue*. Cambridge: Cambridge University Press, 2018.

Kidd, Erika. "Book IV: Fugitive Beauty." In *Augustine's Confessions and Contemporary Concerns*, edited by David Meconi, S.J., 73–90. St. Paul, MN: Saint Paul Seminary Press, 2022.

———. "The Drama of *De magistro*." *Studia Patristica* 98, no. 24 (2017): 133–39.

———. "In the Beginning: Wittgenstein Reads Augustine." In *Augustine and Wittgenstein*, edited by John Doody et al., 37–56. Lanham, MD: Lexington Books, 2018.

———. "Making Sense of Virgil in *De magistro*." *Augustinian Studies* 46 (2015): 211–24.

———. "Parting Words: Augustine on Language and Loss." *Ramify* 6, no. 1 (2017): 59–83.

King, Peter. "Augustine on the Impossibility of Teaching." *Metaphilosophy* 29, no. 3 (July 1998): 179–95.

Kirwan, Christopher. "Augustine's Philosophy of Language." In *The Cambridge Companion to Augustine*, edited by Eleonore Stump and Norman Kretzmann, 186–204. Cambridge: Cambridge University Press, 2001.

Kries, Douglas. "Virgil, Daniel, and Augustine's Dialogic Pedagogy in *De Magistro*." In *Nova Doctrina Vetusque: Essays on Early Christianity in Honor of Fredric Schlatter, S.J.*, edited by Douglas Kries and Catherine Brown Tkacz, 139–52. New York: Peter Lang, 1999.

MacCormack, Sabine. *The Shadows of Poetry: Vergil in the Mind of Augustine*. Berkeley: University of California Press, 1998.

Mackey, Louis. "The Mediator Mediated: Faith and Reason in Augustine's 'De Magistro.'" *Franciscan Studies* 42 (1982): 135–55.

Madec, Goulven. "Analyse du *De magistro*." *Revue d'Études Augustiniennes et Patristiques* 21 (1975): 63–71.

Marion, Jean-Luc. *In the Self's Place: The Approach of Saint Augustine*. Translated by Jeffrey Kosky. Stanford, CA: Stanford University Press, 2012.

Martini, Simone, and Lippo Memmi. *Annunciation with St. Maxima and St. Ansanus*. 1333, tempera on wood, 184 x 168 cm, The Uffizi.

Matthews, Gareth B. *Augustine*. Malden, MA: Blackwell Publishing, 2005.

———. "Knowledge and Illumination." In *The Cambridge Companion to Augustine*, edited by Eleonore Stump and Norman Kretzmann, 171–85. Cambridge: Cambridge University Press, 2001.

Mendelson, Michael. "'By the Things Themselves': Eudaimonism, Direct Acquaintance, and Illumination in Augustine's De Magistro." *Journal of the History of Philosophy* 39 (2001): 467–89.

Mulhall, Stephen. *Philosophical Myths of the Fall*. Princeton Monographs in Philosophy. Princeton, NJ: Princeton University Press, 2005.

Nawar, Tamer. "Every Word Is a Name: Autonymy and Quotation in Augustine." *Mind* 130 (2021): 595–616.

Nietzsche, Friedrich. "Birth of Tragedy." In *Basic Writings*, translated by Walter Kauffman. New York: Modern Library, 1966.

Oliver, Kelly. "Reading Nietzsche with Irigaray: Not Your Garden-Variety Philosophy." *Journal of French and Francophone Philosophy* 27, no. 1 (2019): 50–58.

Ployd, Adam. "The Place of *De magistro* in Augustine's Theology of Words and the Word." *Augustinian Studies* 54 (2023): 43–56.

Rist, John. *Augustine: Ancient Thought Baptized*. Cambridge: Cambridge University Press, 1994.

Schumacher, Lydia. *Divine Illumination: The History and Future of Augustine's Theory of Knowledge*. Chichester, West Sussex: Wiley-Blackwell, 2011.

Sessa, Kristina. "Christianity and the Cubiculum: Spiritual Politics and Domestic Space in Late Antique Rome." *Journal of Early Christian Studies* 15 (2007): 171–204.

Shanzer, Danuta. "Avulsa a Latere Meo: Augustine's Spare Rib—Confessions 6.15.25." *Journal of Roman Studies* 92 (2002): 157–76.

Skerrett, Kathleen Roberts. "Consuetudo Carnalis in Augustine's Confessions: Confessing Identity / Belonging to Difference." *Journal of Religious Ethics* 37 (2009): 495–512.

Stead, Christopher. "Review of John Rist's *Augustine*." *Journal of Theological Studies* 47 (1996): 316–21.

Teubner, Jonathan D. *Prayer after Augustine*. Oxford: Oxford University Press, 2018.

Vaught, Carl G. *Encounters with God in Augustine's Confessions: Books VII–IX*. Albany: State University of New York Press, 2004.

Vergil. *The Aeneid*. Translated by Sarah Ruden. New Haven, CT: Yale University Press, 2008.

———. *P. Vergili Maronis Opera*, edited by R. A. B. Mynors. Oxford Classical Texts. Oxford: Oxford University Press, 1969.

Wetzel, James. *Augustine: A Guide for the Perplexed*. London: Continuum International Publishing, 2010.

———. "Body Double: Saint Augustine and the Sexualized Will." In *Weakness of Will: From Plato to the Present*, edited by Tobias Hoffmann, 58–81. Studies in Philosophy and the History of Philosophy. Washington, DC: Catholic University of America Press, 2008.

———. "The Oracle and the Inner Teacher: Piecemeal Naturalism." In *Pragmatism and Naturalism: Scientific and Social Inquiry after Representationalism*, edited by Matthew Bagger, 277–96. New York: Columbia University Press, 2018.

———. *Parting Knowledge*. Eugene, OR: Cascade Books, 2013.

Whitford, Margaret. "Introduction" In *The Irigaray Reader*, edited by Margaret Whitford. Oxford: Blackwell Publishers, 1991.

Wittgenstein, Ludwig. *Philosophical Investigations*. Translated by G. E. M. Anscombe, P. M. S. Hacker, and Joachim Schulte. Rev. 4th ed. Chichester, West Sussex: Wiley-Blackwell, 2009.

INDEX

Irigaray on, 43
words and, 6–7, 12–13, 64, 87,
  101, 113
intimacy
  Confessiones on, 56–59, 62–63, 65,
    67–72, 103–7, 126n.11, 130n.17
  with God, 15–17, 49, 65, 70,
    78–80, 84–86, 88, 91, 104–6
  intelligibility and, 18, 56, 69, 93,
    106, 113–16
  Irigaray on, 35–36, 44, 49, 78–80,
    84–86, 88, 90–91
  speech and, 16, 29, 32, 90, 112, 114
Irigaray, Luce
  on Adam and Eve, 78–79
  on Apollo, 43–46
  on Christ, 36, 39, 46–49, 77–78,
    80, 83, 85–91
  on Christianity, 35–39, 43,
    48–49, 78, 86
  on Dionysus, 39–43
  on knowledge, 53
  on language, 35–37, 48, 123n.21
  on Mary, 46–48, 78, 80–85,
    87–88, 90–91
  on Nietzsche, 37–39
  responses to, 123n.6
Israelites, 85
Iulus (*Aeneid*), 22–23, 25

J
Jacob (biblical figure), 79
Jesus. *See* Christ
John the Baptist, 85
Jordan, Mark D., 127n.26
Joseph (saint), 82

K
Kant, Immanuel, 118n.5
Kenney, John Peter, 130n.21
Kenyon, Eric, 117n.1 (intro)
King, Peter, 117n.2 (intro)

Kirwan, Christopher, 120n.36
knowledge, 6, 42, 47, 84, 87, 115
  Augustine on, 5, 8–11, 31–32, 54,
    57, 60–62, 66, 69, 72, 96, 98,
    100
  God and, 10–11, 15, 56–57, 63,
    72, 74, 79, 83, 86, 101
Kries, Douglas, 121n.11

L
Lacan, Jacques, 38
language, 11, 14, 43, 48–49, 86–87,
  89, 112–13, 121n.10
  Augustine on, 19–33, 55–56, 66,
    74, 100–103, 106, 112–14,
    119n.20, 120n.36, 121n.1,
    121n.10, 122n.13
  De magistro on, 13, 16, 19–33,
    55–56, 74, 99–103, 112–13,
    119n.18, 119n.20
  Irigaray on, 35–37, 48, 123n.21
  poetry and, 22
  understanding and, 5, 31, 97,
    102–3, 132n.8
  Wittgenstein on, 12, 18
  See also speech; words
Latin language, 28, 66, 96, 101, 103,
  117n.2 (intro), 129n.5
  literature in, 16
  translation of, 4, 117n.2 (intro),
    122n.20, 125n.5, 127n.28
Levinas, Emmanuel, 38
lightning, 40, 42–43, 103
lions, 30
logos, 18, 89
love
  Augustine on, 25, 32–33, 43,
    55–57, 59, 67, 69–72, 101,
    111–16, 126n.11
  of Christ, 78, 101–2, 106, 115
  of God, 46, 49, 59, 70, 72, 74,
    81–82, 101–2, 111

ERIKA KIDD is an associate professor of Catholic studies at the University of St. Thomas.